Understanding Art Education through the Lens of Threshold Concepts

Educational Futures

RETHINKING THEORY AND PRACTICE

Series Editor

Michael A. Peters (*Beijing Normal University, P.R. China*)

Editorial Board

Michael Apple (*University of Wisconsin-Madison, USA*)
Tina Besley (*Beijing Normal University, P.R. China*)
Gert Biesta (*University of Edinburgh, UK*)
Liz Jackson (*Educational University of Hong Kong, Hong Kong*)
Jian Li (*Beijing Normal University, P.R. China*)
Gary McCulloch (*London Institute of Education, UK*)
Mark Olssen (*University of Surrey, UK*)
Fazal Rizvi (*University of Melbourne, Australia*)
Susan Robertson (*University of Cambridge, UK*)
Linda Tuhiwai Smith (*University of Waikato, New Zealand*)
Arun Kumar Tripathi (*Indian Institute of Technology, Mandi, Himachal Pradesh, India*)
Eryong Xue (*Beijing Normal University, P.R. China*)

VOLUME 75

The titles published in this series are listed at *brill.com/edfu*

Understanding Art Education through the Lens of Threshold Concepts

By

Matthew Ravenstahl

BRILL

LEIDEN | BOSTON

Cover illustration: Photograph by Heather Warstler

All chapters in this book have undergone peer review.

The Library of Congress Cataloging-in-Publication Data is available online at https://catalog.loc.gov

Typeface for the Latin, Greek, and Cyrillic scripts: "Brill". See and download: brill.com/brill-typeface.

ISSN 2214-9864
ISBN 978-90-04-50810-1 (paperback)
ISBN 978-90-04-50811-8 (hardback)
ISBN 978-90-04-50813-2 (e-book)

Copyright 2022 by Koninklijke Brill NV, Leiden, The Netherlands.
Koninklijke Brill NV incorporates the imprints Brill, Brill Nijhoff, Brill Hotei, Brill Schöningh, Brill Fink, Brill mentis, Vandenhoeck & Ruprecht, Böhlau Verlag and V&R Unipress.
All rights reserved. No part of this publication may be reproduced, translated, stored in a retrieval system, or transmitted in any form or by any means, electronic, mechanical, photocopying, recording or otherwise, without prior written permission from the publisher. Requests for re-use and/or translations must be addressed to Koninklijke Brill NV via brill.com or copyright.com.

This book is printed on acid-free paper and produced in a sustainable manner.

Contents

Foreword IX
    Julie Rattray and Ray Land
Preface XV
List of Figures XX

1 Introduction 1
  1 Identity and Self 4
  2 Affective Dimension 6
  3 Ethical Implications of This Book 7
  4 Art as Knowledge 9

2 State of the Art: Art Education in the Twenty-First Century 17
  1 Philosophical Underpinnings and Implications for Art Education 18
  2 Art as a Discipline and Content 20
  3 Visual Culture and Visual Literacy: Implications for Art Education 22
  4 Semiotic Theory in the Art-Learning Environment 25
  5 The Farce of Being Color-Blind: Equity, Culturally Responsive Teaching, and the Relevance of Positionality 28
  6 The Issue of Student-Centered Engagement and Equity 30
  7 Art Education or Glorified Coloring 32

3 Threshold Concepts 37
  1 Threshold Crossing and Characteristics of Threshold Concepts 37
  2 Liminality 40
  3 Affective Dimension of Liminal Space and Art as a Vehicle for Navigation 43
  4 The Involvement of the Affective Dimension and Liminality in Learning Environments 46
  5 Transformative Theory 49
  6 Troublesome, Tacit, and Ontological Knowledge and the Liminal State 50
  7 Visual Art as Insight into the Experience of the Liminal State 51
  8 Boundedness and Boundary Objects 53

9   Discursive Element and Visual Art: Linguistic and Nonlinguistic Knowledge and Self-Dialogue   55

10   Conclusion   57

4   Jayden: A Split Self   62

1   Introduction   62

2   Jayden   62

3   Jayden's Artwork and the Liminal Space   69

4   Jayden's Art Portfolio   71

5   Aline: "I'm Just Hoping I Can Stop Surviving and Start Living"   81

1   Introduction   81

2   Aline's History, Artwork, and Finding of Voice   83

3   Aline and the Liminal State   89

4   Institution and Healing   91

6   Rene: A Conversation with My Subconscious   99

1   Introduction   99

2   Rene's Portfolio   99

3   Rene and the Navigation of the Liminal Space and Threshold Crossing   109

4   Semiotic Dialogue: Communication, Expression, and Voice   111

7   Cade: "Because I Don't Care What You Think"   114

1   Introduction   114

2   Identity and Self   115

3   Crisis and Troublesome Knowledge   117

4   Cade: "Because I Feel Like the Voice Is Definitely a Big Part of Myself and Who I Am"   118

5   Cade's Art Portfolio   122

6   Cade's Liminal Experience and Discursive Elements   130

8   Discussion and Conclusion   133

1   Introduction   133

2   Visual Art and the Complex Threshold Concept of Self and Voice   134

3   Visual Art Navigating the Affective Dimension and the Stuck Place   136

4   Visual Art as Semiotic Dialogue   138

5   Pedagogy Informed by Semiotic Theory   140

CONTENTS VII

6 Engaging with Liminality and Psychological Safety 144
7 Implications for Curriculum and Learning in the Visual Art Classroom 147
8 Assessment of Learning in the Art Environment 148
9 Implications for Education Policy and Learning Environments 149
10 Consideration for Future Research and Recommendation for Art Education 152

Index 155

Foreword

Julie Rattray and Ray Land

This is a rich and generative time for arts-based research and education. Arts-based approaches in recent decades have forged new modes of imagining and conceptualizing the ways in which we enact and understand teaching, learning, and educational research. With this new book Matt Ravenstahl takes this field of scholarship forward in creative and important ways, drawing attention to the transformative and healing potential of arts-based education and the complex positionality it entails for artists/learners and teacher/researchers.

This book builds constructively on this recently emergent field. Maxine Greene (1995) has pointed out the distinct role the arts can play in opening up understanding through encounters with the unimagined and the uncertain. Tom Barone (2001, p. 24) has made a rallying call for an expressive research that can involve play and exploration, which can "endow features of our experience with more than a single meaning." Others, such as Richardson (2000) and Mullen (2003), envisage research assuming a performative, provocative, even poetic nature. We will see all these tendencies enacted within this interesting volume.

Significant dimensions within Matt's book, derived from his interest in "threshold concepts," are those of troublesome knowledge, liminality, and identity. In this, his work resonates with the approach characterized by Irwin and De Cosson (2004) as "a/r/tography," or what they term "rendering self through arts-based living inquiry." A/r/tography, they suggest,

> is an inquiring process that lingers in the liminal spaces between *a(artist)* and *r(researcher)* and *t(teacher)*. Entering into a/r/tography arises out of a "desire and daily life" (Rasberry, 2001, p. 1) to make sense and create meaning out of difficult and complex questions that cannot be answered in straightforward or linear tellings. The issues in question may permeate a life and engage emotional, intuitive, personal, spiritual, and embodied ways of knowing – all aspects of one's private, public, and/or professional self (Springgay and Irwin, 2004). (Springgay et al., 2005, p. 902)

They emphasize that such living enquiry is an embodied encounter, as we witness in the artistic productions of many of Matt's student cases, rather than merely visual or textual representation. Such inquiry often takes the form of "interrogations" in the course of which "difference and contradiction ask viewers/readers to reexamine assumptions, destabilizing forms of identification," inspiring "thoughtful action" and entailing a "complex and multifarious act of meaning making" (ibid., p. 903). There are, however, risks involved in such approaches: "Loss, shift, and rupture are foundational concepts or metonyms for a/r/tography. They create openings, they displace meaning, and they allow for slippages. Loss, shift, and rupture create presence through absence, they become tactile, felt, and seen" (ibid., p. 898).

Matt Ravenstahl, in his own teaching and research, does not shy away from such risk-taking. The student experiences documented here – of Jayden, Aline, Rene, and Cade – present narratives of fractured identities, conflicted histories, and a search, through art making, for authentic voices. They involve personal reinvention, reconstitution, healing, and well-being – all promoted through a search for *clarity*. This is work with strong purpose, both pedagogical and developmental. Matt argues that "education can establish newfound relevance and substantively contribute to the holistic development of students (in the education context) by embracing the epistemic nature of visual art" (Ravenstahl, this volume). His experience is testimony that "many students represent powerful experiences and feelings in their artwork as well as profound shifts in their states of being or conceptual clarity." It is a work, also, with strong and commendable ambition, "to empower art educators to understand this epistemic element as well as to inform our own pedagogical approaches and learning environments." This concern with the self-development and healthy reconstitution of younger learners reflects earlier studies, such as Stephanie Springgay's examination of adolescent experiences of the body in (and as) visual culture in her Canadian study *Inside the Visible: Youth Understandings of Body Knowledge through Touch* (2004). Her artistic exploration of relationality through installation and video-based art foreshadows the powerful accounts offered in this volume. A similar concern for healing through artistic exploration can be found in an earlier application of the threshold concepts framework and liminality theory to art therapy with cancer patients by Caryl Sibbett and William Thompson (2008). Their recognition of what they term "nettlesome knowledge" in their students' often difficult search for clarity and personal transformation has been a direct influence on the present volume. The notion of nettlesome knowledge (Sibbett, 2006):

> comprises elements of knowledge that are deemed taboo in that they are defended against, repressed or ignored because if they were grasped they might "sting" and thus evoke a feared intense emotional and *embodied* response. The sting of nettlesome knowledge can make us uncomfortable and so it can be stigmatised. (Sibbett & Thompson, 2008, p. 229)

FOREWORD XI

It might be argued, of course, that such an unflinching pursuit of clarity through artistic self-examination has been a strain throughout art history. Our art historian colleague at Durham, Dr. Anthony Parton, suggests that a large percentage of artworks represent or express aspects of artists' lives with which they were (or are trying) to deal at any one point in time. This would not be a feature of, say, ideologically driven art movements (e.g., Russian constructivism, British or French realism of the mid-nineteenth century) or artworks (e.g., Picasso's *Guernica*). Nor might portraiture, commissioned works of art, or religious art fit his category. However, Dr. Parton points out, self-portraits, such as those of Rembrandt, were and are often used as a means of negotiating one's life journey.

> The thing about the Rembrandt self-portraits is that they begin with him as a young man and the portraits tell you all you need to know: he is young, cocky, a rake, and a lad about town. But then, the moving thing about the Rembrandt self-portraits is this: as he gets older, he uses self-portraiture to reflect on his life journey, on the experience of pain, suffering, loss, and increasing decrepitude. The last portraits are moving entirely because they tell us so eloquently, in pictorial form, of his feelings about being an old man, about life's contradictions, difficulties, and sadnesses.[1]

In his own teaching he uses Rembrandt's *Self-portrait at the Age of 63* (National Gallery, London) to encourage his students to develop their ways of seeing.

> I tell them that I first saw this portrait at their age, at 18, and I walked past it! Now, at the age of 61, I sit and I look because that face is mine. You can see in it the frustrated hopes, the impoverishment, the unattained dreams, the suffering and, above all, shortness of life – there is no time left for Rembrandt, where did it go? Where has my life gone since I first saw that portrait? I can get off on it a bit in the lecture theater and, two years ago, I got carried away looking at the PowerPoint reproduction and talking about it from my perspective. I concluded by saying, "I am that old man." I actually briefly forgot I was meant to be doing a lecture – I turned around and found two students crying!

Parton refers to such artistic processes as "art as cathartic sublimation." In the modern period much of the work of Van Gogh and Cézanne might be seen as autobiographical. Van Gogh's *The Night Café* (Yale University Art Gallery, Connecticut) deals directly with his feelings of exclusion and ostracism from the local community of Arles in the South of France, whereas other works are tackled at one remove, which is where the element of "sublimation" arises. This might take the form of Van Gogh's frequent themes on the suffering of Christ as a metaphor of his own suffering which is, for him, "Christ-like." His landscape *Olive Trees* (Scottish National Gallery of Modern Art, Edinburgh), with its tangled and angst-ridden brushwork, clearly references Christ's suffering in the Garden of Olives and employs biblical themes and references to explore, explain, and understand his own inner feelings and conflicts. Another search for clarity.

Cézanne uses the subject of still life for similar purposes. "The fruit that most frequently appears in his work is the apple," Parton comments. "[It is] a symbol of temptation, forbidden pleasures, but also of judgment, which is used to reference his own erotic and sexual urges." Often the fruit is represented alongside a castrated bust of Eros (impotence), as in *Still Life with Plaster Cast of Amor* (1895, Courtauld Institute Galleries, London) or a classical sculpture of the *écorché*, the flayed man (an image of suffering). Meyer Schapiro (1979), the leading twentieth-century art historian, in his ground-breaking essay "The Apples of Cézanne" (1968), contends that for Cézanne still life is not merely a still life but that for him art provided a cathartic release of instinctual energies which, because of his intense moralistic upbringing, he felt he could not express in any other way, such as through normal sexual relations. "He was, in effect," Parton adds, "the tempted yet castrated Eros who was forever placed in the condition of suffering, like the flayed man."

A new perspective was brought to confessional art in the contemporary period by Tracey Emin's controversial installation *My Bed* (1998, Saatchi Gallery, London). It was conceived during a depressive period following a bad relationship breakup that had culminated in a four-day bedridden bender in which she consumed nothing but alcohol. "When Emin finally left her sheets," Cohen (2018) observes, "she examined the mess she'd created. Crumpled tissues, period-stained clothing, cigarettes, empty vodka bottles, a pregnancy test, lubricant, and condoms surrounded her bed. She decided it was a work of art." Cohen suggests that this example of assemblage art can be construed as a kind of crime scene.

> Viewers can read the component pieces like detectives, reviewing forensic evidence. Yet *My Bed* also elicits warmer, more personal responses. It remains one of contemporary art's most striking depictions of vulnerability, a self-portrait that doesn't veer from the messiness of depression and heartbreak. In particular, it appealed to viewers who connected their own painful experiences to those implied by Emin's installation. (Cohen, 2018)

The student artworks in Matt Ravenstahl's fascinating study possess this same striking quality of vulnerability and pain, but similarly allied to a powerfully forensic quality of self-analysis that opens up vistas of self-recognition and understanding and the possibility of reinvention and transformation.

This book makes a unique contribution and finds an important place in the threshold concepts literature. Not only does it successfully demonstrate how the threshold concepts framework can be productively employed as a tool of art education and research, but it also extends the thresholds framework itself through its drawing attention to the ways in which art making can act as a site of liminal struggle and as a vehicle of personal transformation. The complex positionality of the art maker, the researcher, the teacher, and the learner in this undertaking opens up significant and rich new avenues of educational research and curriculum design approaches. Matt names what he knows with authority and demonstrates in this volume his extensive knowledge of art-making processes as well as the sensibilities, vulnerabilities, strengths, and potential of his students. The chapters that follow offer fresh perspectives and insights that are engaging, enriching, and, at times, disquieting. We welcome its contribution to threshold concepts scholarship and unreservedly commend it to you.

Note

1   Private communication from Dr. Anthony Parton, February 2021. We are indebted to Dr. Parton for his generous sharing of insights drawn from his wealth of expertise and experience in art history education.

References

Barone, T. (2001). Science, art, and the predispositions of educational researchers. *Educational Researcher, 7*(30), 24–28. https://doi.org/10.3102/0013189X030007024

Cohen, A. (2018, July 30). Tracey Emin's "My Bed" ignored society's expectations of women. *Artsy*. https://www.artsy.net/article/artsy-editorial-tracey-emins-my-bed-ignored-societys-expectations-women

Greene, M. (1995). *Releasing the imagination: Essays on education, the arts, and social change*. Jossey-Bass.

Irwin, R. L., & De Cosson, A. (Eds.). (2004). *A/r/tography: Rendering self through arts-based living inquiry*. Pacific Educational Press. https://doi.org/10.1177/1077800405280696

Meyer, J. H. F., & Land, R. (2003). Threshold concepts and troublesome knowledge (1): Linkages to ways of thinking and practising within the disciplines. In C. Rust (Ed.), *Improving student learning theory and practice – Ten years on* (pp. 412–424). Oxford Centre for Staff & Learning Development.

Meyer, J. H. F., & Land, R. (2005). Threshold concepts and troublesome knowledge (2): Epistemological considerations and a conceptual framework for teaching and learning. *Higher Education, 49*(3), 373–388. https://doi.org/10.1007/s10734-004-6779-5

Mullen, C. (2003). Guest editor's introduction: A self-fashioned gallery of aesthetic practice. *Qualitative Inquiry, 9*(2), 165–181. https://doi.org/10.1177/1077800402250927

Rasberry, G. W. (2001). *Writing research/Researching writing: Through a poet's I.* Peter Lang.

Richardson, L. (2000). Introduction – Assessing alternative modes of qualitative and ethnographic research: How do we judge? Who judges? *Qualitative Inquiry, 6*(2), 251–255.

Schapiro, M. (1979). The apples of Cézanne: An essay on the meaning of still life. In M. Schapiro, *Modern art: 19th and 20th centuries: Selected papers* (pp. 1–38). George Braziller.

Sibbett, C. H. (2006). Art therapy in cancer care: Revelatory expression and inclusion of liminal and taboo issues. In D. Spring (Ed.), *Art in treatment: Transatlantic dialogue* (pp. 124–142). Charles C. Thomas Publisher.

Sibbett, C., & Thompson, W. (2008). Nettlesome knowledge, liminality and the taboo in cancer and art therapy experiences: Implications for learning and teaching. In R. Land, J. H. F. Meyer, & J. Smith (Eds.), *Threshold concepts within the disciplines* (pp. 227–242). Brill.

Springgay, S. (2004). *Inside the visible: Youth understandings of body knowledge through touch* [Unpublished PhD thesis]. University of British Columbia. http://resolve.library.ubc.ca/cgi-bin/catsearch?bid=3276873

Springgay, S., & Irwin, R. L. (2004). Women making art: Aesthetic inquiry as a political performance. In G. Knowles, L. Neilsen, A. Cole, & T. Luciani (Eds.), *Provoked by art: Theorizing arts-informed inquiry* (pp. 71–83). Backalong Books.

Springgay, S., Irwin, R. L., & Kind, S. W. (2005). A/r/tography as living inquiry through art and text. *Qualitative Inquiry, 11*(6), 897–912. https://doi.org/10.1177/1077800405280696

Preface

I know that many dedicated educators around the world foster relationships with young people that make education meaningful and, in some cases, feasible. One could argue that the informality of the art-learning environment and the making of art can intensify the personal nature of the teacher-student interactions which impact the students as well as the educator. As a result, we, as educators, should be willing to reflect on these experiences and how they can begin to inform our understanding of the art-making experience and its role in the education of young people.

A few years ago, I worked with a young woman whom I will refer to as Ramesha for the sake of anonymity. Ramesha was born in Sri Lanka but raised in the United States, and there were distinct cultural differences between her home and her social world at school or with friends. Central to these cultural distinctions was the perceived role and identity of women with which Ramesha experienced contradictions. In other words, in her social world, Ramesha felt accepted, appreciated, and treated with equality, but at home Ramesha noticed she was obligated to her home in different ways than her brother. She had to do dishes and clean while he held no obligations to the home. She was told that her duty as a young woman was to marry a Sri Lankan man and make him happy. Observations such as this resulted in a form of troublesomeness relating to her sense of identity and self as a young woman. As a result, Ramesha began to attract relationships that were unhealthy.

As the year progressed, Ramesha continued making art that was indicative of struggles with self-esteem and self-worth, such as skulls or bodies in a tormented gesture. These artworks were trite and lacked a compelling visual resolution. It was Ramesha's trust in me and our conversations about her struggles with relationships and at home that allowed me to understand the purpose of her artwork. As I became familiar with this deeper context, I was able to introduce Ramesha to relevant media (for her): specifically, the found objects and the media of installation. It was in the construction of an installation for her IB visual art exam that I observed profound change in Ramesha's work and her ontological state.

"You know what, Mr. Ravenstahl? I realized I don't need a man to be happy." "You know what, Ramesha. I think you just graduated high school." This is an exchange that occurred as Ramesha was completing her installation which allowed me to reconsider art education by considering epistemic issues, pedagogy, and the art-learning environment. Her change in perspective suggests a relationship to the learning process that, I argue, is much more relevant and important to life than the performance on the IB exam (or any exam, for that matter). Ramesha experienced a resubjectivity by accessing previously inaccessible thoughts and feelings (Land et al., 2005) which coincides with profound change in the visual representation and clarity of her visual language. She evolved a more personal visual language and sophisticated representation of the affective elements related to her experiences. One may construe the change in Ramesha's perspective with implications toward future actions as a transformative experience (Mezirow, 2000), which informs a fundamental question for this book: What relation does the art-making process have to the ontological and visual transformation of meaning? In other words, what role did the art-making process have in her transformation as a young woman?

Positionality, in qualitative research, is often associated with the racial, cultural, gender, sexual, religious, or other identities of the researchers and the participants. It is concerned with the potential relevance of the similarities or differences of these positions and their impact in the research process. England (1994) states that research is a dialogic process that is equally impacted by the researched as well as the researcher. In addition, Milner (2007, p. 388) "rejects practices in which researchers detach themselves from the research process, particularly when they reject their racialized and cultural positionality in the research process." While I certainly adopt positionality conducting research for this book, I have found it also applies to pedagogy and the fostering of relationships with students.

Although positionality as a construct is discussed in the context of research methodology, I argue there are many parallels to pedagogy and the classroom context. In short, students (or individuals who function as subjects in research) "should be treated like people and not as mere mines of information" (England, 1994, p. 82) to be exploited by the teacher or researcher as the neutral collector of facts, which is most applicable when one thinks about assessment. Whether one thinks about standardized testing or performance on art assessments, we (myself included) can forget about the importance of relevance of student learning that informs or engages their life experience. Instead, we can emphasize the making of products (artwork) that are formulaic and conducive to positive assessment on AP or IB exams. This is not to say that highly personal and relevant artwork cannot score well on exams, but there are many instances where performance is the emphasis and we like to presume self-expression and meaning is an inherent part of that process.

The primary attributes that underpin the learning environment in which I teach are my experiences as an exhibiting artist involved in the creative process, my personal struggles with addiction and journey to sobriety, and my intensive theoretical work in pursuit of my EdD. Like many art educators, most of my educational background focuses upon studio art and I have an extensive exhibition record, in various galleries as well as a list of reviews in various news and art publications. I believe the relevance of serious involvement in the art-making process, for art educators, is that it provides some depth of understanding of engagement in the creative process with its affective and cognitive elements. This can translate to pedagogy that goes beyond prescribed tasks based on skill and more toward an actual student engagement in the creative process. When introducing myself to new students, I commonly use this statement: "I am not an art teacher; I am an artist who loves to teach." This philosophical view underpins pedagogy and drastically changes the learning environment from art class to a studio experience. In other words, I do not approach art education as something where I attempt to generate preconceived results from students. Rather, I attempt to foster a personal understanding of the art-making process as a means of expressing and arriving at meaning. The previous discussion of Ramesha is implicit in the idea of visual art as a means of engaging relevant life experience. Furthermore, there are many educators who employ this philosophy to varying degrees.

This is not to say that just because a person is involved in the art-making process they automatically possess an innate ability to be an effective educator. We all know or have experienced teachers who are impressive artists but horrible educators. The art of pedagogy is separate and a unique element, but for an art educator, their pedagogy can and should be informed by their knowledge of the creative process and the power of this experience. Embracing this reality may empower us to place less emphasis on ensuring quality student products by prescribed lessons or controlling methods and focusing on fostering student engagement in an authentic creative and art-making process relevant to life experience. This book presents four case studies that present intense experiences of young people who had this opportunity. Later chapters will introduce and offer in-depth documentation of their journeys of engaging profound and complex life experience through their art-making processes.

My position as an artist is also fueled by my openness about my struggles with alcohol and drugs well into adulthood. Although I have been sober for over ten years, I did not get sober until the age of 35. As is the case with many sober alcoholics, this is considered a positive attribute and I often introduce aspects of learning about living a sober life to students. Whether it be a personal conversation or class discussion, there are many principles of sobriety that would benefit anyone. However, it is important to explicate that my discussion with students about addiction and sobriety do not focus on my sordid adventures (I do not discuss my past with students), but rather the focus is on me as an individual who requires constant involvement in a program that assists in the process and navigation of complex and powerful affective elements.

To be more specific as to the issue of positionality, there are two points to be made. The first is that my background includes intimate involvement with the creative process and human struggle which are integral to my pedagogical approach. These experiences are frameworks which inform my perceptions of student work and often invite open dialogue and create an emotionally safe environment within which one may feel empowered to engage with troublesome knowledge. I often say to students that my openness is an act of fairness in the sense that I am asking them to be vulnerable. It is only fair that I do so in return. The second and perhaps more important point lies in Peter Vivian's (2012) description of crossing a conceptual threshold. Vivian (2012) describes the experience as moving through a dark tunnel and toward light. When one considers this as a form of metaphor, we can associate personal feelings and experiences with this visual description. As a result, one can argue this understanding of threshold crossing seems particularly visceral and relevant within this research. In the specific case of Jayden, Aline, Rene, and Cade (the case studies of this book introduced later), I may not have the ability to completely understand how it feels to experience their darker moments but the journey to sobriety does allow me to understand struggle, mental anguish, and despair. I argue, from my experience, that this shared understanding gives us a means for genuine communication, trust, and a faith in my understanding of moving toward light. I believe all educators hold this capacity because of their life experience, but some feel uncomfortable in perceiving it as a strength. Some feel they are doing something wrong by relating to students on a personal level. Obviously, we are not trying to be friends and I am not seeking that. In fact, many of my students hold a level of respect and value my genuine concern for their well-being as a mentor or caring adult in their life.

References

England, K. V. (1994). Getting personal: Reflexivity, positionality, and feminist research. *Professional Geographer*, 46(1), 80–89.

Land, R., Cousin, G., Meyer, J. H. F., & Davies, P. (2005). Threshold concepts and troublesome knowledge (3): Implications for course design and evaluation. In C. Rust (Ed.), *Improving student learning: Diversity and inclusivity* (pp. 53–64). Oxford Centre for Staff & Learning Development. https://www.ee.ucl.ac.uk/~mflanaga/ISL04-pp53-64-Land-et-al.pdf

Mezirow, J. (2000). Learning to think like an adult: Core concepts of transformation theory. In J. Mezirow & Associates (Eds.), *Learning as transformation: Critical perspectives on a theory in progress* (pp. 3–33). Jossey-Bass.

Milner, H. R., IV. (2007). Race, culture, and researcher positionality: Working through dangers seen, unseen, and unforeseen. *Educational Researcher, 36*(7), 388–400.

Vivian, P. (2012). *A new symbol based writing system for use in illustrating basic dynamics* [Unpublished PhD thesis]. Coventry University.

Figures

4.1 A page from Jayden sketchbook discussing her differences in skin tone. 64

4.2 A page from Jayden's sketchbook about a memory of her grandfather making racist remarks about her. 67

4.3 A page from Jayden's sketchbook about a memory of being called an "oreo". 67

4.4 A page from Jayden's sketchbook that lists racial stereotypes and comments she encountered. 68

4.5 "Blackface" mixed media on poster boards. 72

4.6 "Nigg" double sided mixed media artwork on poster board. 73

4.7 "Inner Warrior" mixed media on paper. 74

4.8 "Jazzy Resentment" mixed media on paper. 74

4.9 "Killer of" mixed media on paper. 74

4.10 "Two Faced" paint on paper. 75

4.11 "Better" mixed media on paper. 75

4.12 "Purity" hemp glued to paper. 76

4.13 A page from Jayden's sketchbook discussing hair as an important element in racial identity. 76

4.14 "Black Transformation" stills from a 2:24 video of Jayden applying paint to her face, neck and shoulders and then removing it. 77

5.1 "Institution" view of the finished installation. 82

5.2 "Institution" detail shot of the markings on the inside. 82

5.3 A page from Aline's sketchbook recalling some difficult experiences in a mental health hospital. 84

5.4 A page from Alines sketchbook reflecting on her suicidal thoughts and cutting. 85

5.5 A page from Aline's sketchbook reflecting upon her lack of faith in the mental health system. 85

5.6 A graphite drawing executed in Aline's sketchbook and submitted as part of her portfolio. 86

5.7 Film stills from a video that depicts a peace symbol made of being incinerated. 88

5.8 "Institution " view of the completed installation. 93

5.9 Detail views of "Institution". 94

6.1 "Untitled" is a life size painting comprised entirely hand prints on paper. 101

6.2 Details of "Untitled". 102

6.3 Mural that is painted in the main hallway of our school which depicts two female figures facing each other. 104

FIGURES

6.4   Detail of the mural that depicts positive and negative attributes overlapping.   104

6.5   Found object sculpture that uses an actual door with a cast of Rene's hand in place of the door knob.   106

6.6   A sculpture of two hands reaching toward each other. The lower hand is wounded and reaching for help while the upper hand is reaching down.   108

6.7   Digital photograhs of Rene meant to capture her feelings about her sense of self.   108

7.1   Installation created by Cade during his freshman year of high school and incorporated his body.   120

7.2   Overall views of Cade's final IB exhibition.   123

7.3   Drawings made of marker on paper.   124

7.4   "Creeping Shadows" is made of cut paper and is reminiscent of the installation Cade created in ninth grade.   125

7.5   "Non Verbal" is a plaster sculpture that depicts a mouth with words on the tongue.   126

7.6   "Snap" is comprised of a mouth and ear made of ceramic clay that are connected by twine that is frayed.   127

7.7   "Held In" is acrylic on two pieces of canvas that comprise the shape of a mouth.   128

7.8   "Breakthrough Performance" consists of the physical remnants and a video documentation of a performance piece in which Cade smashes a door and tries to repair it.   129

7.9   Video still from "Breakthrough Performance" where Cade is hitting the door with a sledge hammer.   129

CHAPTER 1

Introduction

With this book I intend to provoke reflection and a rethinking of art education through the lens of threshold concepts research (Meyer & Land, 2003, 2005, 2006). The preface provides some context for my commitment to understanding relationships between threshold concepts and the visual art-making process, but I hope to establish a clear basis for this interest in this chapter. I argue that art education can establish newfound relevance and substantively contribute to the holistic development of students (in the education context) by embracing the epistemic nature of visual art. I am confident that art educators around the world have taught young people as they undergo a form of transformation that was documented in, or in some way associated with, artwork that they (the student) created. I have seen how many students represent powerful experiences and feelings in their artwork as well as profound shifts in their states of being or conceptual clarity. These powerful moments are indicative of the visual art-making process empowering epistemic movement toward a more developed self that may involve healing or clarity. I am writing this book to empower art educators to understand this epistemic element as well as to inform our own pedagogical approaches and learning environments. As a result, I believe this can facilitate more students to experience transformative and powerful learning experiences apart from the isolated who that are desperate or blessed.

The threshold concepts theoretical framework and relevant constructs will be addressed in a substantive manner in Chapter 3, but a brief introduction will be beneficial at this point. Meyer and Land (2006) describe threshold concepts as the crossing of a conceptual portal that is often troublesome in nature, which is characterized by a transition through a state of liminality. Liminality is often described as a transformative state or a "liquid space with great potential for learning, experimentation and growth" (Felten, 2016, p. 5). The description of crossing a conceptual portal requires it to be "approached, negotiated and perhaps experienced as a transition in terms of sense of self" (Meyer & Land, 2006, p. 19). To paraphrase, the crossing of thresholds generally involves knowledge that is troublesome and the reconciling or understanding of this troublesome knowledge involves the crossing of a threshold. However, the journey of threshold crossing often involves the holistic self, engaging the cognitive and affective dimensions and resulting in a transformed ontological state. Therefore, I tend to prefer to describe threshold crossing as a journey because it involves powerful learning that is transformative and involves struggle.

© KONINKLIJKE BRILL NV, LEIDEN, 2022 | DOI:10.1163/9789004508132_001

There are two key points implicit in this brief description of threshold crossing that are integral to this book and art education. First, threshold concepts originally focus upon improvements in learning and understanding which might give rise to improved performance, but I argue that art education is about human development. In other words, art education can offer much more than domain-specific learning such as developing technical skill or mastery of visual design. In my experience, the art-making process can act as a catalyst for personal transformation and I argue that the case studies in this book represent situations where the art-making process was an essential form of knowledge construction due to the complex affective elements tied to the individuals' experiences. Therefore, in this book the crossing of thresholds involves a change in subjectivity or self (Meyer & Land, 2003, 2005). Second, the brief description of threshold crossing involves the approaching and negotiation of a liminal state which in the domain of art education highlights the relevance of semiotic theory (De Saussure, 1959; Brandt, 2004). The art-making process can function as a unique semiotic vehicle and assist in the navigation of complex liminal spaces (Ravenstahl & Rattray, 2019; Ravenstahl, 2018). This book focuses upon this epistemic value of visual art making as nonlinguistic knowledge (Langer, 1957) with the intention of clarifying this potential for art education in the twenty-first century.

Ideally, this brief description of threshold crossing and liminality presents the potential that I am sure many of us have experienced in our classrooms. In other words, the essential challenge I wish to present to myself and the global art education community is honest reflection upon pedagogy and the nature of learning in our classrooms. Moreover, the conscious consideration of providing a learning environment, experiences and assessments that foster engagement or the provocation of the liminal state. I intend for this book to introduce the threshold concepts theoretical framework as a lens for us to reflect upon the nature of student engagement with the art-making process. More specifically, I ask: Do our students remain subject to demonstrations of skill or cookie cutter projects or do they employ the art-making process as a means of navigation and engagement with profound ideas or experiences? Many art educators understand the visual art-making process is more than aesthetic production and it is a means of engagement with the world. However, this does not mean we facilitate learning in our classrooms in a manner that is consistent with this belief. I am in no way aiming (nor will I attempt) to provide strategies for teachers to replicate, but I will seek to promote the understanding of the epistemic potential of the visual art-making process.

A common assumption that I have encountered in my years as an art educator is that education in the arts fosters critical thinking in students. While

I agree this is a possible outcome it is often accepted as a generalized claim. Unfortunately, this undermines important distinctions that can and should be made in the pedagogies, learning environments, and learning in different art classrooms around the world. Consequently, there is little nuanced understanding of what teaching and learning in the arts means, especially by those not directly involved in the field (Davis, 1993). This often includes administration, parents, school boards, and, I would venture to say, many art educators and their students. As a result, the reality of the role of art in education is that it has become "nice but not necessary" (Eisner & Day, 2004, p. XI), which is compounded by the accountability movement and standardized assessment.

The accountability movement in US education has placed emphatic value on the ability to quantify learning in classrooms and has prioritized value upon core academic subjects which threatens the role of art education in schools (Heilig et al., 2010; Eisner, 2001). On the one hand, this promotes an isolated world in which art educators are specialists that have a unique position in a school that could enrich the educational experience of many young people. On the other hand, this unique role can allow the art educator to remain comfortably on the fringe of the school subjects and faculty where there is little need or interest in challenging their methods or role in the education of young people. This specialist status can fuel an incestuous approach to thinking about art pedagogy and the full potential education in the arts provides our schools and young people. "Conceptually, art education has become something of a goldfish bowl floating in a larger sea of issues and considerations. The world within the bowl is not invalid or unrealistic, but it is not cognizant of wider, equally relevant horizons" (Nadaner, 1984, p. 26). The argument being made is that there are ways art making is understood and utilized in the art world, academic research, and psychology (to name a few) that many in our world of art education are either ignorant or unwilling to engage and enrich our classrooms. I believe that engaging the epistemological elements of art making can establish the necessity of art education in public education in the twenty-first century.

In this book I document four case studies of students whom I taught in an advanced visual art course in my public high school. The case studies document the liminal journey of the students as a basis for reflection upon the art-making process. More specifically, the case studies provide a thick and rich (Geertz, 1973) representation of how these four students used the art-making process to navigate the liminal space that has profound affective involvement. Two of the young people experienced sexual abuse, one young woman struggles with racial identity, and one young man comes to terms with his sexual orientation. The case studies provide entire art portfolios that represent in a visual manner the navigation of the liminal space and ontological shifts within the young people. The case studies also involve excerpts from sketchbooks and interviews where each of the young people describe their experiences and how the art-making process was an essential element in their ability to process and heal the self. By presenting the case studies this book makes inferences toward the value of art education in the twenty-first century, as well as provoking critical reflection upon the art-learning environment, curriculum, and pedagogy.

In this chapter I have provided a brief orientation to threshold concepts which is a theoretical underpinning of this book. In Chapter 2 I will examine relevant issues in the state of art education and their relationship to threshold concepts. As a result, I hope to establish a substantive discourse and consider their relevance to the threshold concepts framework. In Chapter 3 I will provide a more in-depth description and discussion of threshold concepts. The case studies in Chapters 4 through 7 are included to provide emotive examples of students who employed the art-making process for something more than performance on assessment or skill development. The final chapter will address implicit and relevant questions for art educators and the classroom. The remainder of this introductory chapter will establish and conceptualize two underpinning theoretical elements that are inherent in the reality of considering visual art within the threshold concepts theoretical framework. The constructs of identity and self are core to this book in that they function as thresholds which characterize the associated liminal journey for each of the young people. Therefore, this chapter will take the opportunity to conceptualize these constructs as they are relevant and core to each of the case studies presented. In addition, this chapter will provide a discussion of art as knowledge and inherent epistemic qualities associated with visual art. This discourse is important as this book and the way I present threshold concepts assumes inherent epistemological elements in the art-making process.

1   Identity and Self

The constructs of identity and self are integral to understanding the thresholds or portals crossed by the individuals in the case studies. Moreover, identity and self represent the origins of troublesomeness for the young people and conceptualize their respective liminal journeys due to profound experiences that involved trauma in some cases. The literature provides many variations defining the constructs of identity and self (i.e., Lapsley, 2004; Maslow, 1967; Rogers et al., 1978); furthermore, the literature is explicit in the shortcomings of existing understandings of these constructs and the need for constant evolution of their meaning (Fearon, 1999). The reason I am discussing these constructs in the introduction (as opposed to a later chapter) is due to their significant and integral role of understanding the case studies and the nature of the cognitive and affective elements involved in their journey of threshold crossing. In other words, the constructs of self and identity are threshold concepts for the individuals in the case studies and I hope this book unfolds for readers the implicit complexity of threshold crossing relevant to constructs of this nature. While I am introducing these constructs as threshold concepts here, I will further address the understanding of self and identity as complex or thorny thresholds in Chapter 3 as well as in the discussion chapter. It is also important to highlight that I am not interested in making an original contribution to the literature of identity and self. Rather, I wish to pull from established theories to effectively conceptualize the constructs for the reader. In recent years issues of gender and identity have become increasingly complicated and numerous perspectives have been presented that further challenge our existing understandings (i.e., De Beauvoir, 1953; Sedgwick, 2015). It is not my intention to engage in this discourse.

Well-established conceptualizations of identity argue the formation of identity is a social construction with a relationship to the perception of others (Erikson, 1968; Fearon, 1999). In other words, our formation of identity can be influenced by the community around us and understanding how those individuals define us or our ability to better understand our identity in recognizing differences from those around us. Therefore, the internal experience of one's identity in relation to the external social reality can conflict with the more internal experience of identity (Fearon, 1999). Elements of identity can be considered physical or genetic traits that one may "feel powerless to change, or which in their experience they cannot choose, such as sexual orientation or membership in a social category" (Fearon, 1999, p. 23). Obviously, our physical or genetic identity is often easily identified by individuals who inhabit our social world, which makes us subject to assumptions which may conflict with our internal understanding of our identity.

This discussion highlights an important distinction between identity and self. The internal experience of "'my identity' is not the same thing as my *feelings* about my self" (Fearon, 1999, p. 10), which is a more consistently internal and private understanding as opposed to the more socially influenced understanding of identity. There are stronger emotions attached to our understanding of self (than what is labeled "non-self") and it is only through these subjective feelings that the self can be identified (Cooley, 2011; Brewer & Gardner, 1996). This may seem obvious at first, but when taken into consideration with identity based on physical and genetic traits this individuated self becomes important. In other words, the self can be understood as "the totality of an individual's thoughts and feelings having reference to himself as an object" (Gecas, 1979, p. 7), which distinguishes one from others who may share certain characteristics.

"There can be no argument but that the subjective feeling state of having a self is an important empirical phenomenon that warrants study. Like many other phenomena, the subjective feeling of self tends to be taken for granted until it is absent" (Epstein, 1973, p. 2). This book and the case studies intend to provide the reader access to the students' liminal experience with their sense of self and how the art-making experience facilitates an ability to cross relevant thresholds. Felten (2016) argues the need for threshold literature to take greater account of the students' perspectives, especially regarding the navigation of the liminal state and how this journey impacts individuals. The case studies intend to provide a unique glimpse into the role of the affective dimension and the art-making process which can promote empathy and understanding in the readers.

2 Affective Dimension

There have been efforts in educational research and specific policy (in the United States) that prioritizes or at least places emphasis upon the student experience regarding learning. For example, culturally responsive teaching, equity, and trauma-informed classrooms. In my opinion, research and policy that prioritizes relationships between the student's affective state and learning is generally good for educators and schools to consider. However, we ultimately come back to define learning as a cognitive process that is assisted by positive feelings or experiences in the school environment. This is also a positive thing for schools and educators to consider. In my experience, there is a gap in understanding the role of the affective dimension in learning and it is separated from and arguably a lesser consideration than the cognitive dimension. In short, learning is generally accepted to be a cognitive process, which I am not trying to debate. However, clearly there are important aspects to the affective dimension and learning that exceed simply being in a more positive ontological state.

In the context of the art-learning environment, emotion and the affective dimension are integral to the learning experience. In many cases one could argue that art is a representation of emotion but is not necessarily the experience of emotion. Furthermore, one can argue that learning in art is domain specific and even the affective elements involved in the art-making process

INTRODUCTION

are more related to interest than they are to learn in art and that the cognitive gains are what's important.

However, I argue that when students can engage the art-making process as having inherent epistemic potential the learning process becomes more reliant upon the affective dimension. The case studies in this book experienced ontological shifts and were able to negotiate complex life experiences by coming to terms with and navigating and affective liminal experiences. Eventually, the students demonstrated cognitive changes, specifically with language and an ability to accept aspects of themselves they were previously incapable of doing. Based upon these experiences, I argue that in the context of this learning environment the students involved both the affective and cognitive dimensions of the art-making process. But the navigation of a complex affective liminal space was the essential aspect of their transformative experience. In this context, the affective dimension takes on a very important role.

My interest in threshold concepts lies in the way art education can be understood as an epistemic process that can act as a vehicle for negotiating complex affective thresholds.

3   Ethical Implications of This Book

The young people who provide the case studies for this book are anonymized for the purpose of protecting their identity. As previously stated, these are all young people whom I have taught in advanced art courses in my high school over a span of several years. At the time of my writing of this book each of these young people have granted their enthusiastic permission for me to write about their experiences and to present their respective art portfolios, writing, and excerpts from interviews that I conducted with each of them in private. All the young people signed consent forms and willingly participated in the interviews and research process. The students gave a second consent, as young adults over the age of 18, when I notified them of the writing of this book. The students (unrelated to this book) willingly exhibited their work in public galleries during the time of this research, which demonstrates a willingness to present sensitive and personal experience in a public forum. Despite the overwhelming enthusiasm to share their private experiences there are immediate ethical questions which require explication. The case studies focus on four high school students: Jayden, Aline, Rene, and Cade.

Jayden is a female of mixed race, born of an African father and a German mother. She was adopted as an infant by a Caucasian (white) family with whom she has lived her entire life. Jayden has lived in diversely different areas of the United States before moving to my area and attending high school where I teach. Jayden struggled with issues of racial identity her entire life due to various experiences and the diversity of areas where she has lived.

Aline, a white female, lived in several different areas of the United States. Aline also suffered sexual abuse as a young child. The abuse was inflicted by her father's friends and it is unclear (to me) if her father participated or only was aware of the crimes but remained complicit. Aline holds deep resentment toward her mother because she told her mother of the abuse and her mother instructed her never to speak about it. Because of these experiences, Aline suffered immense psychological and emotional turmoil, turning to self-harm and cutting as a means of addressing her suffering. She was hospitalized on several occasions and has undergone many intense residential treatment programs. At the time of our working together, Aline was no longer in residential treatment and had been free from self-harm and cutting for some period. She was still seeing a therapist, although she openly said she was not honest in sessions, and she was voluntarily living with her father, despite their history, as she felt her mother was too dysfunctional.

Rene is a white female who lived her entire life in the area where my high school is located. Rene suffered sexual abuse as a young child, well before she attended high school. The abuse was discovered, and legal and therapeutic remedies were pursued. The lasting impact of the abuse seems to impact issues of self-esteem and has led to depression.

Cade is a white gay male who struggled with issues of identity and self. More specifically, Cade had experienced intimate feelings or attraction toward other males and was able to acknowledge these to an extent. However, he tried to explain these feelings away as a phase or something that would simply go away on its own. Cade experienced profound psychological and emotional distress as he began to realize that homosexuality was not something that was going to simply go away on its own. He struggled with accepting this as an element of his sense of self and identity.

It is essential to point out several key issues regarding the ethics of working with Jayden, Aline, Rene, and Cade. Even though two of these students shared an art class (the third was in the following period) they were not aware of each other's histories or that each was participating in the research. Cade was several years behind, in school, from the other students. The selection of these individuals for inclusion in this research arose from each of them beginning to address complex issues in their artwork completely independent of me. In other words, it is through the artwork and their explanations of it that I became aware of their deeper concerns and troubling experiences. I did not ask them to make art about prior difficult experiences; each of them felt safe enough to use the class structure to express these issues, in the context of their artwork.

INTRODUCTION

I had worked with two of the girls for a year or more (in the context of different art classes) and one of them for several months before they began expressing the content relevant to this research. I had taught Cade for three years and his journey had slowly unfolded over the entirety of his time. He eventually remade an artwork from an earlier time that he realized was the origins for his liminal journey. At different points these young people began to demonstrate ontological shifts in relationship to the respective content of their artwork. I found these shifts compelling and worth documenting and thinking about in a more substantive manner. This book is a result of those efforts.

Unfortunately, in my many years of teaching it has not been uncommon to discover there are multiple students per class who have had similar experiences in their past. As a result, I am well versed in "county procedures" and have an established routine in implementing them. In short, when such situations occur, I walk with the student to the school psychologist and sit with the student while the relevant history is revealed. This is done in a nonthreatening manner but usually requires discussion as to the need to reveal the nature of the artwork being made by the student. I also call each parent and alert them to the content of the student's work and the fact that the school clinical team is aware of the situation. As a result, the parents had an awareness as to my working with the students. In my experience, this awareness allows for a freedom for the student and me to talk about the artwork with a safety net in place in case the student becomes overwhelmed or troubled while working. Although this did not happen during this research, there have been occasions with other students where a breakdown has occurred during class periods. When clinical teams and parents are aware, as previously mentioned, there is no hesitation on anyone's part to support the student as needed.

It is also essential to point out that the nature of our work together is not an attempt to conduct therapy sessions. In the case of Aline and Rene, I do not know many of the details of the events that occurred in the past and we did not spend time discussing them. The research focused entirely upon their artwork and its relationships to these troubling experiences. While I am sure there is some therapeutic value to the student's engagement with the art-making process, it was neither a motive nor a concern of this research. This book is concerned with the nature of each of the individual's engagement with visual art and its ability to navigate troublesome knowledge and the liminal space.

4 Art as Knowledge

"The arts-based researcher may persuade readers or percipients of the work to revisit the world from a different direction, seeing it through fresh eyes, and thereby calling into question a singular, orthodox point of view" (Barone & Eisner, 2012, p. 16). This quote articulates the core aims of this book and the presentation of case studies with the intention of provoking art educators to reflect upon their pedagogical approach in the context of threshold and semiotic theories. The use of the case studies presents an interrelationship of liminal experience and the art-making process. The power of this documented journey may empower other art educators to reflect upon the potential of their own learning environments and reconsider the purpose of art education.

In the important first chapter of Knowles and Cole's *Handbook of the Arts in Qualitative Research* on "art and knowledge," Eisner (2008) begins by asking the question: Are the arts merely ornamental or do they have a more significant role in human understanding? The answer is that they do both – and the classroom context dictates the conceptualization for students. More specifically, the pedagogical approach will obviously underpin the learning environment and, therefore, the nature of student engagement in a relationship of art and knowledge. Therefore, as previously stated, the aim of this research is to provoke educators into reflection upon the breadth and depth of visual art to far exceed the limitations of being merely ornamental.

According to McNiff (2008, p. 29), "[a]rt-based research can be defined as the systematic use of the artistic process, the actual making of artistic expressions in all the different forms of the arts, as a primary way of understanding and examining experience by both researchers and the people that they involve in their studies." Barone and Eisner (2006, p. 96) argue that a primary purpose of arts-based research in education is to "persuade the percipient to see educational phenomena in new ways, and to entertain questions that might have otherwise been left unmasked." Furthermore, Langer (1957) argues there are discursive and nondiscursive forms of knowledge, which is an important issue in this research, namely the consideration of visual arts as nondiscursive knowledge. However, the commentators already cited, as well as others (i.e., Barone & Eisner, 2012; Leavy, 2015; Bagley & Cancienne, 2002), generally think of the value of nondiscursive knowledge as a means of enhancing research to being internalized by readers. However, the aspect of visual art as being nondiscursive knowledge is important to research of liminal space as it applies to learning in the arts and knowledge construction that encompasses the affective as well as the cognitive elements.

Arts-based research results (in part) from the work of Langer (1957) that helped establish the cognitive element of the arts in the academic context "and established the intellectual basis for approaching art making as serious inquiry" (McNiff, 2008, p. 30). In addition, Eisner states (2008, pp. 5–6) that "knowledge and understanding are not always reducible to language" and argues that "words are proxies for direct experience." Implicit in this view is the limitations of language as semiotic signs that may often lack the capacity to effectively represent the complexity of human experience and feeling, whereas employing nonlinguistic or (in the case of this book) visual signs may more effectively represent and express the nuance of subjective meaning and experience. From the perspective of the researcher, arts-based methods, in this research, take form as visual data and a semiotic dialogue that occurs within the learning environment. In one sense the arts-based methods provide us with a unique opportunity to glimpse the affective experience of the liminal journey. In another sense it can be considered an invaluable tool for teaching and learning in the arts. The visual art-making process can help address the limitations of words regarding the case studies and the feelings associated with them. This is particularly relevant since the liminal state can involve a difficulty in the formation of linguistic signs as a means of communicating or processing troublesome knowledge (Land, 2014).

The role of arts-based research, within this book and in general, is not to reach conclusions but rather to raise questions or possibilities for understanding issues more deeply (Barone & Eisner, 2012; Leavy 2015). As previously stated, visual arts provide a unique lens through which to glimpse the liminal state. However, to this point, we may come to understand aspects of the affective and cognitive elements within the liminal state. Susanne Langer (1957, cited in Barone & Eisner, 2012, p. 9) states that "arts-based research is not a literal description of a state of affairs; it is an evocative and emotionally drenched expression that makes it possible to know how others feel." The visual art-making process can make an important contribution to the threshold concepts literature in that it provides a unique means to glimpse the liminal experience from the student perspective. This understanding is both an empathic understanding of its difficulty and potential impact of the learners' experience but also the navigation of the liminal space. This is due to the visual art-making process serving to make the internal and emotional empirical, providing understanding through different forms of representation.

As presented in the example of Ramesha, there are potential relationships implicit in visual art production and the engagement of troublesome knowledge and the threshold framework. This exploration is not concerned with conclusions which further argue art is a form of knowledge (as opposed to ornament) but rather builds upon the dense theoretical literature that establishes this as a truth (Barone & Eisner, 2012; Dewey, 1934; Eisner, 2008; Langer, 1957; Leavy, 2015; McNiff, 2008). The significance of this point is that the research-based and established relationship of art and knowledge suggests an inherent ability of visual art to navigate liminality and cross thresholds through nondiscursive and affective knowledge. Therefore, implicit in this inquiry, visual art functions in multiple roles and is viewed through the lenses of educational subject as well as the product of expressive activity, a research method and form of data. Therefore, this research is contingent upon the student engaging with the visual art process as an opportunity to convey experience and construct knowledge in a manner that is authentic to real-life experience, making it relevant within the threshold framework. As a result, this allows for the transformative aspect of the work to be received in a more personal and profound manner (Knowles & Cole, 2002) as the percipient can engage the liminal journey of these young people and associate them with their own experiences in classrooms. Sullivan (2004, pp. 795–796) argues that "making art and interpreting art become the basis for constructing theories of artistic knowing" and educational research that "merely borrow[s] research methods from other fields denies the intellectual maturity of art practice as a plausible basis for raising significant theoretical questions, and as a viable site for applying important educational ideas." The point being made is that the consideration of visual art making in the context of the threshold concepts framework can provoke educational researchers to understand the inherent epistemic potential for effective use. There is potential in the consideration of visual art as a contribution to the threshold concepts literature as a methodology as well as a vehicle for navigating the liminal space. The inherent characteristics of visual art that are prevalent in the arts-based research literature establish the epistemic value of the domain, which can offer a unique glimpse into the much-needed student experience of liminality.

Patricia Leavy (2015) describes the value of arts-based research by referring to her own experiences as an academic. She encountered frustration with more traditional forms of research about the limitations of representation in the context of ethics and accessibility by an audience. I argue it is essential for the reader/viewer to experience a young persons' liminal journey along with them as opposed to only locating coded excerpts within an existing theory. Leavy (2015, p. 2) argues that the arts-based approach allows for the effective representation of content while generating "empathic understanding, self-reflection and longer lasting learning experiences for readers." More specifically, Knowles and Cole (2002, p. 208) describe a dissertation on child sexual abuse that is presented as poetry which gives insight into the issues related to trauma but allows us access through the affective lens of the lived experience. Bagley and Castro-Salazar (2012) argue that art's primary purpose is to provide an audience with evocative access to multiple meanings, interpretations, and voices associated with lived diversity and complexity. In other words, research may often address issues that fall outside the scope of the reader, but art-based approaches can make them accessible. Arts-based methods can provide the deliteralization of knowledge which opens the door for other modes of knowing whose truth is important to uncover and represent (Eisner, 2008). At the heart of this is a distinction between expression and statement where "science states meanings; art expresses them" (Dewey, 1934, p. 84). Barone and Eisner (2012, p. 3) argue the expression of meanings empowers percipients of arts-based research with a "heuristic through which we deepen and make more complex our understanding of some aspect of the world."

The form of representation of the research can assist in expanding the knowledge base and challenging assumptions regarding learning in art classrooms to a wider audience of art educators less interested in purely theoretical literature. However, academics interested in the threshold framework may find the research further introduces arts-based approaches which may offer insight into highly relevant constructs and our ability to understand them. In both instances visual art is employed as a means of seeking and representing human experiences and perspectives. In the context of this book, the art-making process is not only a mechanism for students to engage with the liminal state, but the same art allows us to empathically participate in the student journey itself. The linguistic data provides context but the artwork itself provides a means for us to experience an exchange of subjectivity with the cases presented. It can be argued that this perspective can produce research that provokes reflection and insight that can address the arguable stagnation of art education.

McNiff (2008) discusses a danger of arts-based research as the reality that the work can become a form of self-indulgence (of the researcher) and the meaning or value of the work getting lost. In this context, it is important that I do not become more interested in presenting quality artwork made in my class instead of issues related to art education understood through the lens of threshold concepts. The mere correlation of art and research does not make it arts-based nor valuable research (Bagley & Cancienne, 2002; Bagley, 2008; Bagley & Castro-Salazar, 2012). In other words, we must avoid presenting "a delightful poetic passage or a vivid narrative that does little educational work" (Eisner, 2008, p. 23). In this book the use of the case studies and the focus on the art-making process are meant to provide insight into educational issues related to threshold concepts and the navigation of the liminal space.

The discussion on arts-based methods highlights the epistemic benefits inherent in the visual arts which holds implications for the richness of data. Part of the relevance of this discussion also directly relates to research in threshold concepts and the domain of arts education. "Visual media's contribution derives mainly from the ability of images to facilitate and enrich communication thus enhancing the data" (Pain, 2012, p. 303). In other words, the affective dimension and liminal experience is given form in moments of navigation of the liminal space and transformation. The reflective interviews are literal evidence of linguistic signs of transformation and further explanation of the underpinning thought process of the young people. The epistemic role of visual art making is another profound source of knowledge that is unique and directly generated from each of the young people. The implications of this methodology can also hold implications for art-learning environments and be a source of reflection upon pedagogy. Chapter 2 will highlight relevant issues in art education regarding pedagogy and learning environments with the intention of establishing relationships between art education and threshold concepts.

References

Bagley, C. (2008). Educational ethnography as performance art: Towards a sensuous feeling and knowing. *Qualitative Research, 8*(1), 53–72.

Bagley, C., & Cancienne, M. B. (Eds.). (2002). *Dancing the data*. Peter Lang.

Bagley, C., & Castro-Salazar, R. (2012). Critical arts-based research in education: Performing undocumented historias. *British Educational Research Journal, 38*(2), 239–260.

Barone, T., & Eisner, E. (2006). Arts-based research in education. In J. Green, G. Camilli, & P. Elmore (Eds.), *Handbook of complementary methods in education research* (pp. 95–111). Erlbaum.

Barone, T., & Eisner, E. W. (2012). What is and what is not arts based research? In T. Barone & E. W. Eisner (Eds.), *Arts based research* (pp. 1–12). Sage. https://www.doi.org/10.4135/9781452230627.n1

Brandt, P. A. (2004). *What is semiotics? The briefest overview ever seen.* https://sociosemiotics.net/files/whatissemiotics.pdf

Brewer, M. B., & Gardner, W. (1996). Who is this "We"? Levels of collective identity and self-representations. *Journal of Personality and Social Psychology, 71*(1), 83–93. DOI: 10.1037/0022-3514.71.1.83

Cooley, C. H. (2011). The looking-glass self. In Jodi O'Brien (Ed.), *The production of reality: Essays and readings on social interaction* (5th ed., pp. 126–128). Sage.

Davis, D. J. (1993). Art education in the 1990s: Meeting the challenges of accountability. *Studies in Art Education, 34*(2), 82–90.

De Beauvoir, S. (1953). *The second sex* (H. M. Parshley, Trans. & Ed.). Knopf.

De Saussure, F. (1959). *Course in general linguistics*. Philosophical Library.

Dewey, J. (1934). *Art as experience*. Putnam.

Eisner, E. W. (2001). Should we create new aims for art education? *Art Education, 54*(5), 6–10.

Eisner, E. (2008). Art and knowledge. In J. G. Knowles & A. L. Cole (Eds.), *Handbook of the arts in qualitative research: Perspectives, methodologies, examples, and issues* (pp. 3–12). Sage.

Eisner, E. W., & Day, M. D. (Eds.). (2004). *Handbook of research and policy in art education*. Routledge.

Epstein, S. (1973). The self-concept revisited: Or a theory of a theory. *American Psychologist, 28*(5), 404–416. doi:10.1037/h0034679

Erikson, E. H. (1968). *Identity: Youth and crisis*. Norton.

Fearon, J. D. (1999). *What is identity (as we now use the word)?* [Unpublished manuscript]. Stanford University. https://web.stanford.edu/group/fearon-research/cgi-bin/wordpress/wp-content/uploads/2013/10/What-is-Identity-as-we-now-use-the-word-.pdf

Felten, P. (2016). Introduction: Crossing thresholds together. *Teaching and Learning Together in Higher Education, 1*(9). http://repository.brynmawr.edu/tlthe/vol1/iss9/1

Gecas, V. (1979). *Beyond the "looking-glass self": Toward an efficacy-based model of self-esteem* [Paper presentation]. The Annual Meeting of the American Sociological Association, Boston.

Geertz, C. (1973). *The interpretation of cultures*. Basic Books.

Heilig, J. V., Cole, H., & Aguilar, A. (2010). From Dewey to no child left behind: The evolution and devolution of public arts education. *Arts Education Policy Review, 111*(4), 136–145.

Knowles, J. G., & Cole, A. L. (2002). Transforming research: Possibilities for arts-informed scholarship? In E. O'Sullivan, A. Morrell, & M. A. O'Connor (Eds.), *Expanding the boundaries of transformative learning: Essays on theory and praxis* (pp. 199–213). Palgrave Macmillan.

Land, R. (2014, July). *Liminality close-up* [Thought paper presentation]. HECU7 at Lancaster University.

Langer, S. K. (1957). *Problems of Art: Ten philosophical lectures*. Scribner.

Lapsley, D. K. (Ed.). (2004). *Moral development, self, and identity*. Psychology Press.

Leavy, P. (2015). *Method meets art: Arts-based research practice* (2nd ed.). Guilford Press.

Maslow, A. H. (1967). Self-actualization and beyond. In J. F. T. Bugental (Ed.), *Challenges of humanistic psychology* (pp. 279–286). McGraw-Hill.

McNiff, S. (2008). Art-based research. In J. G. Knowles & A. L. Cole (Eds.), *Handbook of the arts in qualitative research: Perspectives, methodologies, examples, and issues* (pp. 29–40). Sage.

Meyer, J. H. F., & Land, R. (2003). Threshold concepts and troublesome knowledge (1): Linkages to ways of thinking and practising within the disciplines. In C. Rust (Ed.), *Improving student learning theory and practice – Ten years on* (pp. 412–424). Oxford Centre for Staff & Learning Development.

Meyer, J. H. F., & Land, R. (2005). Threshold concepts and troublesome knowledge (2): Epistemological considerations and a conceptual framework for teaching and learning. *Higher Education, 49*(3), 373–388. https://doi.org/10.1007/s10734-004-6779-5

Meyer, J. H. F., & Land, R. (Eds.). (2006). *Overcoming barriers to student understanding: Threshold concepts and troublesome knowledge*. Routledge.

Nadaner, D. (1984). Critique and intervention: Implications of social theory for art education. *Studies in Art Education, 26*(1), 22–26.

Pain, H. (2012). A literature review to evaluate the choice and use of visual methods. *International Journal of Qualitative Methods, 11*(4), 303–319.

Ravenstahl, M. J. (2018). *Bringing the apple and holding up the mirror – A qualitative study of student engagement in visual art and the navigation of liminal space and transformation* [Unpublished PhD thesis]. Durham University.

Ravenstahl, M. J., & Rattray, J. (2019). Bringing the apple and holding up the mirror: Liminal space and transformation in visual art making. In J. A. Timmermans & R. Land (Eds.), *Threshold concepts on the edge* (pp. 127–142). Brill Sense.

Rogers, C. M., Smith, M. D., & Coleman, J. M. (1978). Social comparison in the classroom: The relationship between academic achievement and self-concept. *Journal of Educational Psychology, 70*(1), 50–57.

Sedgwick, E. K. (2015). *Between men: English literature and male homosocial desire*. Columbia University Press.

Sullivan, G. (2004). Studio art as research practice. In E. W. Eisner & M. D. Day (Eds.), *Handbook of research and policy in art education* (pp. 795–814). Routledge.

CHAPTER 2

State of the Art: Art Education in the Twenty-First Century

In this chapter I provide insight into important discourses on the philosophical underpinnings of the development of art education as well as more recent theoretical concerns that are implicit in art pedagogy and classroom environments. My intention in this chapter is to establish clarity as to the relationships I understand to exist between art education and threshold concepts. I wish to be clear that I am not trying to present an overall historical account (i.e., Efland, 2017) of the development of art education nor present the wide range of theoretical issues that exist in education today and apply them to the arts in a broad sense (i.e., Chalmers, 2004; Eisner & Day, 2004). More specifically, I am being selective in issues that I have come to perceive as relevant to the field of art education and have association with the threshold concepts theoretical framework and its ability to inform meaningful reflection upon pedagogy, learning environments, and assessment.

This chapter will present discourse as to the content of art education that evolves out of the work of Lowenfeld (1947) and Dewey (1934) and what can be called an expressionist view (Efland, 2017) of art education, as well as Eisner (1972) and Barkan (1955) and their argument about art as a discipline. These philosophical views of art education present a conceptual space in which to discuss and elaborate issues relevant in art education, despite the fact there are other large frameworks worthy of discussion. This book is focused upon the lens of threshold concepts and its connection to pedagogy and the value of learning experiences in visual art. Therefore, I will discuss the epistemic aspects of the art-making process framed in the perception of art making as a means of fostering critical thinking skills. Theoretical issues such as visual literacy, student-centered engagement, as well as equity and diversity education are also discussed in the context of pedagogy, the art-learning environment, and the art-making experience.

Finally, the accountability movement in US education (Heilig et al., 2010; Berliner, 2009; Eisner, 2001), as previously discussed, is a deeply concerning and ongoing issue for art educators regarding the role of the arts in twenty-first-century education. This chapter and this book are underpinned with concern about the impact this movement has had upon art education. Samuel Hope (2004) asserts that the relevance of research in art education must address

© KONINKLIJKE BRILL NV, LEIDEN, 2022 | DOI:10.1163/9789004508132_002

the health and survival of the field. The accountability movement and laws such as the No Child Left Behind Act (2001) have unapologetically prioritized standardized testing and core academic subjects. Berliner (2009) argues that curriculum design in these recent years laud the notion of closing the gap in achievement but, overemphasizes the quantified data of standardized testing and removes the more enriching aspects of education, such as the arts. In turn, the value of the arts and the role of art education has become challenged. I argue that art educators are not necessarily making this situation any better. As art educators, we need to fully understand the potential of art making in human development and public education and adjust our pedagogies to instill this value in our learning environments. However, many of us are limited to repeating the pro arts rhetoric to which we are exposed or comfortably remain on the fringes of the school faculty, using our specialist category to remain outsiders.

Although I do not maintain a consistent discourse on how the accountability movement impacts art education throughout this book, it is important to be explicit that this impact is a driving concern for this research. In this chapter I select philosophical and theoretical issues in art education that I will link to threshold concepts and illustrate their presence in presented case studies. As previously stated, my intention in this book is to provoke reflection upon the role of art education and our respective pedagogy through the lens of threshold concepts. As a result, I hope we can begin to reestablish the value of art education in the twenty-first century through our own authentic pedagogies and passion for the art-making process. In short, I am arguing with this book that reestablishment of the value of art in education will be found in the evolved understanding of the epistemological value of the art-making process.

1 Philosophical Underpinnings and Implications for Art Education

The expressionist point of view was influenced by Lowenfeld (1947) and Dewey (1934), who argued that the purpose of art education was not the art product but the impact of the art-making experience upon the child. In other words, "how he creatively and sensitively applies his experience in the arts to whatever life situations may be applicable" (cited in Efland, 2017, p. 235). Lowenfeld (1947) and Dewey (1934; Read, 1943) argued that creative practice fostered growth components that developed young people into empathic and more broad thinking individuals capable of internalizing varying perspectives. "Introspective accounts of artists and other highly creative individuals had indicated that creativity was intimately associated with an openness to individual experience and exhibited freedom, playfulness, and uniqueness respective to individuals" (Burton, 2009, p. 323). Lowenfeld (1947) and Dewey (1934) believed these growth components impacted individuals in a manner that fostered human development, such as emotional and psychological levels fostering the development of broader thinking and compassionate people.

Simultaneously to emphasizing the expressive freedom of the art-making process upon the child there is less emphasis placed upon the formal aspects of the artwork in comparison to the internal experience of the art-making process. Lowenfeld (1947) argued that input from adults into a child's art or creative output can act as a corrupting influence and the purity of the child's imagination must be preserved. Eisner (1984) validates Lowenfeld and Dewey's view of art education that the tasks in a given classroom should not be beholden to any curricular outcome and should act as an instrument for opportunities to create work that is personal and meaningful without a predetermined outcome for learning but what Dewey (1916) called "vital experience." Learning environments such as this can provide teachers access to the intimate experiences and feelings of their students' lives, resulting in relationships that can enrich the teaching and learning experience.

Lowenfeld's view that education should repair a broken world was clearly intertwined with the context of the postwar era, but critics have since argued his philosophy reduced art education to mere encouragement of free expression (Efland, 2017). There is merit to the criticism of Lowenfeld but context is necessary in order to prevent oversimplification. In my view, art education that is mere encouragement of self-expression can misconstrue expressive process for what is really nothing more than glorified coloring. More specifically, students can mindlessly push materials around with little consideration of the outcome. In some cases, this is a subconscious creative process and in others this is the glorified coloring. Dewey's (1916, 1934) concept of vital experience is relevant to this criticism. In other words, when art education does not involve conceptual and/or affective engagement between the student and the artwork or between the educator and student, then the resulting work and learning may lack substance or purpose. However, vital experience, in education, is activity in which the link between action and consequence is interconnected with previous and future (related) activities (Dewey, 1916). The consequence or end-in-view is still tied to the immediate situation, but the process of inquiry used to reach this end-in-view not only has a connection with, but has been enriched by, previous inquiry in some way (Glassman, 2001).

The point I am making here is that engagement with vital experience involves feeling, experience, concept, or media informed by affective and/or cognitive dimensions, no matter the degree of awareness. In my view, students need guidance and discourse in order to navigate, understand, and develop their expressive interests and personal visual language. This is not to say that significant artworks are not or cannot be made in isolation by young people, but it is important to acknowledge that not every artwork made by a young person results in genuine or meaningful expression.

One unintended consequence of pedagogy is often found to be an overly prescribed focus upon elements and principals of design. This type of learning environment can also lack substance and hinder the ability of students to genuinely engage in the art-making process (Gude, 2004). Eisner suggests that art is a process in which "skills are employed to discover ends through action; whereas craft is a process whereby skills are used to arrive at a preconceived end" (cited in May, 1993, p. 212). When students are confined to experiencing art only as a demonstration of skill, they can be deprived of the transformative opportunity of art making as a launching point or stepping-stone for discovery. More specifically, the prescribed learning environment often leads toward a successful but prescribed aesthetic result, but may often prevent students from truly experiencing the epistemic potential of the art-making process or developing the ability to experience the art-making process as a form of non-linguistic knowledge construction.

In summary, the expressionist underpinning toward education makes the important fundamental argument that the art-making experience must be authentic to the individual. And there is a need for educators to understand the important distinctions between instructing and facilitating, telling and discussing. In my experience, it is essential to understand when students are floundering or producing aimlessly as compared to struggling to engage the cognitive and affective dimensions.

> Only by wrestling with the conditions of the problem at first hand, seeking and finding his own way out, does he think. [...] In such shared activity, the teacher is a learner, and the learner is, without knowing it, a teacher – and upon the whole, the less consciousness there is, on either side, of either giving or receiving instruction, the better. (Dewey, 1916, p. 188)

2 Art as a Discipline and Content

The work of Barkan (1955) and Eisner (1972) focused upon art as a discipline that maintains its own system of inquiry that is as valid as any science (Efland, 2017). The core assumption of this book – that the art-making process possesses epistemic potential – in further explicated above (in the section called

"Art and Knowledge" in Chapter 1). This notion is associated with the idea of art as a system of inquiry. Although art as a means of inquiry employs methods and processes differently from traditional sciences, the outcomes and knowledge derived from these processes has been utilized and validated in the highest forms of academia for multiple decades (Leavy, 2009, 2015). It was impact of Barkan (1955) and Eisner (1972) that made the historically important step for art in public schools to become a serious part of public education by introducing the concept of curriculum to art education.

Eisner (1979, 1984) defined the term "curriculum" in distinction from "subject matter." Art as a subject matter must be converted into a series of events intended to have educational value. However, Eisner (1985, p. 259) is explicit in stating there is an important difference between "intention and actualization" of curriculum in the classroom. This observation by Eisner is, in my view, an essential point of reflection for art educators and is directly associated with the nature of our learning environments as a result. Every teacher believes their approach or method is the correct one, but this is not the issue or relevant question for us to indulge in as individuals or groups. The relevant question should focus on the effectiveness of our approach to facilitate genuine engagement with the art-making process, whether this be primarily a formal exploration or the use of art as a manner of self-discovery or reflection. The aforementioned "series of events" is referring to lessons, tasks, or units implemented in the art classroom. I argue that a primary concern here is that our approach or implementation of a curriculum should never be limited by the educator's lack of expertise or ability to differentiate instruction. As educators, we should always focus upon the experiences and needs of the students we are teaching and by informed by a certain competence and knowledge in the processes and ideas inherent in the history of art. I have heard many educators start descriptions of their assigned projects with the phrase "I like." Who cares what the teacher likes? Should not the concern be with what it is about the student's experiences or feelings that can be expressed through a visual language that is genuine and authentic? Its appeal to my (or any teacher's) taste is not only irrelevant but it has no place in an educational setting.

In my view, the educator's ability to understand and possess facility in the art-making process is of great importance in the effective implementation of an art curriculum. The reason I argue the significance of this point is that the proportion of prescribed approaches toward actualization of curricular goals is dependent upon the comfort and understanding of art making as knowledge construction versus skill execution. In other words, many art educators understand actualization of curriculum as articulated instructions intended to generate a predictable and predetermined result that is intended to illustrate different aspects of fundamentals of design. Gude (2004) mentions a study by the National Art Education Association (NAEA) which states that the elements and principles of design remain the point of emphasis in art classrooms. I acknowledge that command of fundamental aspects of art making are important, but as inherent aspects to assessing art and points of critique in more personal approaches to art making, and not as the core focus of art courses. "I wonder why what is still considered by many to be the appropriate organizing content for the foundations of [the] 21st century art curriculum is but a shadow of what was modern, fresh, and inspirational 100 years ago" (Gude, 2004, p. 6).

The implication and relevant criticism of the continued emphasis upon the elements and principles of design (Gude, 2004; Ravenstahl, 2018) in the resulting art-making process disregards student engagement with vital experiences or troublesome knowledge. The consequence is students are less likely to experience the transformative and more powerful aspects of learning that are unique to the art-making process and will be limited to domain-specific knowledge. In short, the conceptualization of learning in more prescribed settings becomes a focus upon grades and performance as opposed to learning. The domain-specific and even static nature of art education places the elements and principles of art as a form of truth and end instead of facilitating students to embrace informed choice and reflection in the art-making process (Gude, 2004). This suggests the value of referencing past artwork and formal aspects of art making as a means of research and reference of visual language and representation as opposed to mimicry.

The next sections address constructs and theories that allow discourse that begins to inform a manner of perceiving and understanding an epistemic involvement in art pedagogy. Theoretical literature addressing visual and semiotics can inform a means for art educators to view artwork beyond its formal qualities. In turn, this can change the nature of our student/teacher interactions and learning environments.

3   Visual Culture and Visual Literacy: Implications for Art Education

When we consider visual literacy specifically in the context of visual art, we must begin to consider the vast span of time and culture. The meaning of different symbols or intentions behind art making will have distinct differences based on the culture and time period of origin. Furthermore, different art forms will place emphasis upon emotional or more cerebral intention for expression. Therefore, the use of visual elements will range from more straightforward to subtle or even minimal in visual representation. The point being the construction and interpretation of meaning of artwork requires sound analysis that also embraces the subjective and affective as elements of the individual. I would also speculate that visual literacy is an original form of literacy existing previously to deriving meaning from text. I point to ancient cave drawings (such as the 35,000-year-old painting of a babirusa, or 'pig-deer,' discovered in Indonesia) as evidence for my argument (Aubert et al., 2014). The point here is not to debate what forms of literacy existed first but to highlight the fact that individuals have been deriving meaning from images for millennia. I argue it is important to consider that individuals have felt compelled to represent their experiences in visual signs and symbols for at least 35,000 years (ibid.). The explicit point is that interpretation of meaning and the expression of meaning are arguably fundamental human activity. As art educators, we should be empowered by the significance of this reality and focus upon the art-making process as the expression and interpretation of meaning as opposed to mere aesthetic exercise or ornament, which hold important underpinnings for pedagogy and learning environments.

Visual literacy (Debes, 1969) has been an integral construct in education for several decades. The literature points to an increased significance of visual literacy due to the rapid and immense changes in technology that impact perceiving, thinking, and experiencing the world in the twenty-first century (Jones-Kavalier & Flannigan, 2006). Yenawine (2003) describes the inherent role of visual literacy in society as the beginning of our interaction with our environment beyond the concrete world which is represented in images. This often begins with pictures or simple representations that foster linguistic development. However, these representations become increasingly complex and are open to wider interpretation. Yenawine (1997) makes distinctions in cognition required to construct meaning from differing types of images. For example, a newspaper image and an abstract painting will vary in degree of cognitive involvement and complexity in the making of meaning. "Presumably, the visually literate person can comprehend on various levels whatever he or she chooses" (Yenawine, 1997, p. 1), but this ability requires educational intervention and is not simply a result of exposure. The generalized exposure to advertisements or television may not involve the cognitive engagement required to evolve visual literacy as focused educational intervention. The implication points to an importance of art education in not only developing a functional ability in navigating society but also places emphasis upon the meaning of images beyond their aesthetic qualities.

Coinciding with the inherent role of visual literacy in human activity is the issue of visual culture which highlights the practical and imperative role of art education and benefits to students. The construct of visual culture is the reality of the vast increase and profound integration of images in daily life (Mirzoeff, 2002). It can be argued that imagery is integral to many aspects of our society and arguably has impact upon such essential elements of human development as the creation of identity and the obtaining and exchanging of knowledge (Chaplin, 2002; Duncum, 2001). There is no agreed upon or universal definition of visual culture and many perspectives have been considered regarding its meaning (i.e., Duncum, 2001; Marling, 1994; Morgan, 1999). Wilson (2000) argues the difficulty of defining visual culture is due to its relevance to many fields or domains (i.e., sociology, art, psychology). Bal (2003) considers visual culture from the perspective of questioning it as a discipline and the complexities of such a status. Henderson (1999) considers visual culture as it relates to the act of perception and the objects that are the focus of our perception. Duncum (2001) ultimately argues the importance of considering the meaning of visual culture as it pertains to imagery that is experienced in society and culture from a wide range of sources.

The relevance of this part of the discussion is to highlight the significance of the phenomena of visual culture and its association to visual literacy. More specifically, there is a clearly understood reality as to the inherent and significant role of images in our daily lives (Mirzoeff, 2002) that suggests the importance of nuanced interpretation and understanding as to the intention and meaning of these images. Duncum (2001, p. 101) highlights examples of art educators who no longer have an interest in "studying the art of the institutionalized art world" and instead focus on "studying the more inclusive visual culture." Clearly, the literature points out the importance of the role of images in society and the impact upon our thinking and navigation of the world. In my experience, art education has expanded to include new technologies, such as animations and memes as well as increased public exchange through virtual and social media. I am confident many educators expand the art-making experience in their classrooms while others remain more traditional. The issue of importance is one of visual literacy in developing the perceptive and critical abilities of young people to navigate personal and societal meaning.

I argue this informs art education in several important ways. First, there is an essential role for art education that lies in visual literacy and the cognitive development of young people to decipher and understand the societal meanings with which they are being bombarded. Furthermore, the involvement of visual literacy in art education can extend beyond understanding images associated with the subject of art. It can pertain to students developing the ability to perceive and derive meaning from their own art-making process that can empower engagement with more profound feelings and experiences. In other words, the discourse of visual literacy assumes the individual is interpreting the meaning of images made by others established in history or society, which is obviously an important element in the education of our young people. However, I also argue that there is great value in students interpreting their own images and processes and it is within this aspect that art education finds continued significance in public education. In my experience, when students are encouraged or facilitated to perceive meaning in their own work it can lead to powerful transformative learning as well as deep engagement that makes meaning from experience and emotion. This internal knowledge construction involves both the affective and cognitive dimensions. The following section discusses semiotic theory, which further elucidates this aspect of visual literacy as an internal epistemic process as well as the implications for pedagogy and learning environments.

4 Semiotic Theory in the Art-Learning Environment

Semiotics is commonly understood as the study of signs and symbols that are generated by humans which communicate intentions and/or meaning (De Saussure, 1959; Brandt, 2004). There is a clear conceptual overlapping of semiotic theory and visual literacy, but establishing a clear distinction between the two theories is a difficult task that is not of great relevance to this book. This section attempts to establish a clarity as to the value of educators understanding associations between semiotic theory and visual art. In my view, the literature of visual literacy is underpinned by the assumption of understanding visual art as a subject. In other words, something which we can learn about as opposed to functioning as a way of knowing. What becomes important to understand is students are not always emotionally capable of expressing in linguistic means the ideas, emotions, or experiences underpinning their work. In some cases, students express, in visual modes, very profound feelings or ideas without being fully cognizant of it. Because of this reality I argue it is crucial that we, as art educators, come to embrace the importance of visual literacy and semiotics in the work of our students and the learning environments that we create. When we begin to understand art as a form of knowledge construction, we can facilitate discussions with students that can lead to transformative and powerful learning.

The experience of making and expressing meaning is an internal process that involves the affective and cognitive dimensions. In the context of the art-learning environment, "communication between these individuals (student and teacher) is in the physical domain where the oral, textual and graphic signifiers play their part" (Land et al., 2014, p. 205). In other words, there are limitations to the ability of language and symbols to accurately communicate the internal experience of others and this complexity is an inherent part of art-learning environments and pedagogy. More importantly, for art-learning environments to foster genuine creative development (to which I keep referring), the nature of the meaning constructed in the art process should be complex and layered with strong emotion – whether or not this emotion is associated with the experiences the student is expressing or the feelings of vulnerability that likely accompany an act of sincere expression. As a result, the ability for educators and students to communicate about the work can be ineffective or limited. In the art therapy literature (i.e., Harnden et al., 2004), art making is valued as a means in which individuals can release profound feeling without having to engage in oral communication. Similar to the art therapy literature, I am arguing that our ability to be sensitive and interpret semiotic signs produced by students in their work can be a means to establish mutual understanding for both the teacher and the student. Rather than giving a student a list of needed alterations based on a purely aesthetic lens, we can use it as a vehicle to listen or as a form of dialogue that can inform us as well as empower the student. In addition, there is an empowered freedom for students in that the details of their experience are not overt, but the visual signs allow for a form of questioning and dialogue that can slowly reveal deeper meaning and feeling that had otherwise been unexpressed or processed. This notion of the dialogic element of visual art can also be highly relevant in issues of inclusion and equity, which is discussed in the next section.

Land, Rattray, and Vivian (2014) propose that knowledge of semiotic theory can enhance pedagogical approaches that can account for subjective difficulties with troublesome knowledge. This points to the importance of emphasizing learning over the delivery of instruction (Smith-Shank, 1995), which Dewey (1916) conceptualizes as pragmatism or learning is an active process of engagement with experience. Pragmatism conceptualizes learning as student driven and occurs as engagement with vital experience (Dewey, 1916). The constructs of troublesomeness and liminal space, which (as previously discussed in Chapter 1) are states of knowledge and being that are difficult and even overwhelming (in some cases) for individuals, are inherent elements in the engagement with vital experiences. Therefore, education considered in this context is based on preparing the student not only to face these moments of vital experience but to engage the troublesome feeling and thoughts that may accompany them. The implication for this book is that the student can employ the visual arts to engage with experiences, feelings, and concepts that are troubling but vital to authentic and relevant learning and human development. The role of semiotic theory is one of epistemic value in that the visual signs used in art making can both construct and express knowledge. In the context of the classroom environment educators can become more empathic and aware of student perspectives and/or struggles which this empathic awareness can often open discussion that leads to profound personal discovery for both the student and the educator.

Smith-Shank (1995, p. 235) presents semiotic pedagogy underpinned by two essential concepts of collateral experience and the artificial nature of historically determined boundaries. Smith-Shank (1995, p. 235) argues the necessity of inviting the learners' collateral experience into a learning environment because they bring with them "acknowledged resources" that facilitate making meaning out of new experiences. The premise of this argument is the prior experience of individuals are an invaluable resource that can be applied even in a subconscious manner and the relevance of learning and meaning can be derived from the embracing of these prior experiences.

Smith-Shank (1995) also argues the artificial reality of historically determined conceptual boundaries that are often stringent in educational environments. This notion coincides with the construct of collateral experience since individual learners will possess a wide range of experience and the construction of knowledge and meaning can be highly subjective and nonlinear. Therefore, this more subjective and messy process can extend beyond the more constrained understanding of knowledge within school subject disciplines. As stated earlier, there are deeply held assumptions that all products produced in an art-learning environment involve the act of self-expression. This is not true and art educators can often hold tightly to the constraint of the conceptual boundaries associated with the domain of art to ensure a visually pleasing result for their students. Smith-Shank (1995) articulates an important point in the discussion of prior experience and conceptual boundaries, as it applies to pedagogy. For self-expression and critical thinking to be a part of our classrooms we must empower our students to enlist prior experience and develop visual language that in some cases challenges the preconceptions of ourselves and what student work should look like or represent.

The importance of discussion of visual literacy, semiotics and semiotic pedagogy begins to establish a crucial point of this book that visual art is a way of knowing and there are inherent epistemic qualities that allow art making to transcend exercises in visual design and become transformative in many cases. More importantly, the artwork can be understood and function in the learning environment as more than a product for assessment. When we consider the lenses of visual literacy and semiotics, there is an element of dialogue in the artwork can that empower understanding through both linguistic and nonlinguistic means. Observing a student's work and approaching it by asking questions of the student rather than simply looking for flaws enables us to understand the student on a more intimate level. In turn, the student's educational experience and their engagement with the art-making process can become increasingly genuine.

5 The Farce of Being Color-Blind: Equity, Culturally Responsive Teaching, and the Relevance of Positionality

In the last few decades there have been many programs established and acronyms used in public schools meant to foster greater sensitivity to race/ethnicity, learning differences, and socioeconomic disadvantage. More specifically, there has been a growing appreciation of how differing cultural experiences and socializations may impact the ability for minorities or less typical learners to access quality education. In recent years the terms "equity" (Blankstein et al., 2016) and "culturally responsive teaching" (Howard, 2016; Gay, 2010) have been brought forth, which focus upon providing equal access to success in education for minorities, economically disadvantaged children, and less typical students of many descriptions, including learning differences, sexual orientation, and gender. Unfortunately, these worthwhile endeavors contend with problematic policies that fail to recognize that disparities in quality education are directly impacted by inequality and the opportunities that are implicit in social and economic privilege (Blankstein et al., 2016; Sahlberg, 2011). As previously mentioned, the intentions of equity and culturally responsive education are intertwined with closing achievement gaps (Berliner, 2009), particularly regarding economically disadvantaged and minority students. However, the means of assessment as outlined in Standard of Learning exams (in the United States) and other aspects of education only exploit the impact of growing inequalities by placing increased accountability on schools by raising standards (Fullan & Boyle, 2014).

In my view, issues of equity and culturally responsive teaching are extremely important but often misconstrued to mean we must help make up the gaps with disadvantaged students by giving them more (Blankstein et al., 2016). In my mind, equity and culturally responsive teaching are pedagogical approaches that are meant to allow our classrooms to possess an equality of opportunity that does not exist in other facets of society. When considered in the context of art education, there are inherent aspects of our subject that can exemplify ideal learning environments but, unfortunately, we often perpetuate the unacknowledged disparities implicit in such problems in US education. The rest of this section will discuss culturally responsive teaching and positionality as a means of highlighting important elements of pedagogy that are associated with equity.

Culturally responsive teaching builds upon the prior experiences and knowledge of diverse students and validates their perspective, knowledge, and presence in a classroom (Gay, 2010). This understanding of culturally responsive teaching holds associations with the previous description of semiotic pedagogy and the integral and valued role of prior experiences (Smith-Shank, 1995). When placing value upon prior experiences considered in the context of culturally responsive teaching, there is a validation of the student and authenticity that can develop with the students work and ultimately enrich the learning environment. More importantly, such validation can begin fostering a sense of belonging and opportunity in at least one area of school. Implications of this understanding of culturally responsive teaching is that the exclusion of prior experience (unintentional or not) denies the educator the opportunity to know and ultimately teach toward these varying perspectives (Howard, 2016). We cannot teach that of which we lack knowledge or awareness which applies to student diversity and subject content (Howard, 2016). In my experience, the most common reason educators ignore or fail to consider the diverse prior experience of students is due to a myopic focus on curriculum implementation. In many instances the significance of this point (culturally responsive teaching) does not enter the psyche of the educator or many assume the prior experiences align or do not differentiate from that of their own privileged status. This aspect of assuming all students are similar is highly significant and discussed by Knight (2006).

Knight (2006) presents a poignant and arguably accurate reality of a common version of culturally responsive teaching that is underpinned by color blindness. In other words, many well-meaning (often white) educators who hold perceptions, judgments, and interactions with the belief that race or color doesn't matter. These perceptions and interactions not only involve classroom dynamics but in the context of educator as gatekeeper dictates the nature and lens of the student's exposure and interaction with the curriculum. Knight (2006) terms this common belief system as "(e)raced," which is a disregard of racial identity and prior experiences, more specifically, the lack of acknowledging racial or ethnic differences reinforces the pervasive norm of whiteness. The lack of acknowledgement of racial difference places emphasis upon whiteness as the norm, which impacts the implicit norms of the learning environment in both the cognitive and affective dimensions (Knight, 2006; Howard, 2016). This is not an overt racist act where authority in the building actively discriminates against minority students or "others," but it does perpetuate and reinforce white privilege and whiteness as the norm or ideal (Knight, 2006). This color blindness is often the manifestation of the educator's well-intentioned belief that race does not matter and that all students are capable. People who are talented, intellectually capable, and possess a work ethic are inherent in all subsets of society; however, as Knight (2006) points out, it is important to make the acknowledgement of cultural and racial differences central to our pedagogy. I argue this is most important in art classrooms where emotional safety and belonging are essential aspects in fostering a student's ability to generate authentic and meaningful work. In some instances, educators see culturally responsive education as an "extra" that they will get too if there is time after they have taught the curriculum. I believe this is an important point of overlap with issues of equity in education. More specifically, unique lessons that focus on diversity ultimately promote differences and can arguably further isolate students. Rather, culturally responsive education and equity are intended to promote authentic engagement with learning through the validation and connection to prior experiences and perceptions (Aikenhead & Elliot, 2010; Halagao, 2010).

The argument being made holds associations with the construct of positionality, which was discussed in the preface of this book. Positionality has its origins in the literature of research methodology (i.e., England, 1994), which criticizes researchers who value the role of being detached from their subjects as opposed to embracing their humanity. I believe the discussion on color blindness and culturally responsive teaching is taking a similar stance as the construct of positionality. In other words, as educators we are in a position of power and authority and we dictate the nature of our learning environments by overt and subconscious decisions and interactions. As already discussed, we often dictate the way students experience and engage with the art curriculum, no matter how prescribed or open ended it is. The relevant point is that we, as educators, need to acknowledge our positionalities of gender, social class, race, and other aspects of our experience of the world and account for differences in experience and opportunities. As Knight (2006) argues, an unacknowledged position (especially if we are white) only perpetuates the norm of whiteness and will ultimately impact the equity of the learning environment. This acknowledgement most often is not a literal conversation but rather an awareness that a teacher's position empowers or excludes differences.

6 The Issue of Student-Centered Engagement and Equity

This chapter has attempted to present issues of art education that both hold associations to threshold concepts and provide a discourse for us to reflect on the reality of the art-making process in our learning environments. The potential role art education can be maintained if we rethink our own pedagogy and understanding of our field. The value of this deeper reflection upon the role of art education and pedagogy, I believe, is outlined in the issues I raised regarding current issues in art education and their implicit association with threshold concepts. In short, the discussion regarding expressionist viewpoints and art as a curriculum point to important developments that validate art as a curricular subject that has its own methodologies and means of assessing quality and value. This then turns attention to issues implicit in the epistemic value of art making in the literature of visual literacy and visual culture which establishes dialogic and cognitive aspects of visual art and its importance to the educational experience. However, I argue that the issues of curriculum and literacy can create a stagnation of art education in that the educator can over-value the fundamentals of design and treat art as a subject which can limit art education to technical exercises. The relevant point I make is these cognitive and dialogic aspects inform the idea that art is a way of knowing and a means for students to engage with prior experiences and understand the semiotic aspects of the art-making process and nonlinguistic language. The implication is that art education should treat the art-making process as a verb as opposed to a noun (Eisner, 2008) that can transcend artificial conceptual boundaries and empower authentic expression and critical thought. When we consider these inherent epistemic aspects of the art-making process and their partial establishment in art education, I believe the issue of pedagogy comes into focus. I am arguing that we, as educators, greatly influence the manner of engagement for the student and the art-making process. By embracing and reflecting upon these inherent aspects we can facilitate transformative experiences by empowering students to understand the potential of art to function as a vehicle for engagement as opposed to something to be looked at or a form of replication.

As the literature states (Blankstein et al., 2016), equity is a conscious effort to provide students with what is needed to ensure their equal access to quality education. As previously stated, equity focuses on students with economic disadvantages or learning differences, as well as minorities and individuals who are less typical. Culturally responsive teaching (Gay, 2010) is closely associated with equity and focuses heavily upon racial and cultural differences. I believe the issue of student-centered engagement is integral to issues of equity (within art education) in the sense that it must genuinely involve the student's prior experiences (Smith-Shank, 1995; Gay, 2010). In art education, students can participate and make art, but this is not always the equivalent of engagement and providing access. My point is that the appearance of equity is easily presumed to exist in art classrooms since students all create an original product to some extent. However, equity understood as genuine engagement must be felt and experienced by the student in order to be a reality. In other words, having a diverse class of students all having the same equipment and opportunity to do the same lesson falls short in my mind. I argue the idea of equity involves the opportunity for a student to introduce their feelings and experiences within a classroom no matter how overt or subtle. We, as educators, must develop a means to be sensitive and aware of this visual language and help foster its development. As a result, true inclusion and equity can be achieved in our classrooms.

In my view, the primary issue is the opportunity for engagement in the art-making process that has its origins in an authentic and internal part of the self. This connects to threshold concepts because when we allow for this genuine engagement with the art-making process the arts can function as a semiotic vehicle that navigates relevant life experience, concepts, or feelings. This is the importance of equity and acknowledging the unique and subjective reality of the individuals we teach. Many of the theories introduced in this chapter orient around visual art as a dialogic element for the inner self as well as communication with others. The issues of equity and culturally responsive teaching asks us to take notice of unspoken elements of power and norms that we are all socialized toward and how these elements can impede different aspects of individuals' opportunity to engage in the art-making process. This holds true for less typical learners as well in that in the arts we have an opportunity to understand our students in both linguistic and nonlinguistic means if we can acknowledge differences as a means of teaching the educator how an individual can access the art-making process from an authentic and meaningful place.

7   Art Education or Glorified Coloring

Is art education just "glorified coloring"? (I must credit my wife for this provocative phrase, which resulted from one of our many talks about education.) The point of the phrase addresses what I believe to be one of the primary issues in art education associated with the specialist status of its instructors. I have argued in this book that the specialist status of art educators can be an effective way for us to avoid full participation in the education process and be able to do things our own way because few others in our buildings have the specialized knowledge we possess. This can allow us to grow stagnant or believe we know how things should be done as opposed to evaluating and reflecting for growth. Where the distinction between art education and "glorified coloring" comes to light is how we design and operate our learning environments. In my experience, many art programs have a selection process that requires students to have jumped through hoops or be given permission to take certain courses. How many of our art students will make quality art as defined by the fundamentals of design and skill, no matter the nature of the learning environment? In other words, the phrase "glorified coloring," in my mind, can refer to us serving students who are inherently skilled at art, thus enabling us to exploit that skill to create work that wins prizes and allows us to feel good about ourselves.

In this reality of art education, we (the educators) are the most guilty of making our contribution to education irrelevant as well as perpetuating inequality in education. In my view, we are not trying to produce artists. We are educating young people through the art-making process and the most relevant learning that results may well transcend the boundaries of visual art. If we limit access to our courses to only those students who demonstrate a certain ability, then we make ourselves irrelevant and participate in education that is a form of making ourselves feel good by working only with those we deem worthy. To make my position perfectly clearly: art education should be about the student's engagement in a meaningful and genuine process, whether the final product be visually impressive or not. I believe we need to facilitate the artistic struggle of our students and even take the journey with them in many cases. In my experience, when we facilitate genuine engagement, students ultimately create sophisticated work that can even exceed expectations. The reason for this is the students have an opportunity to understand their visual language and how their art-making process leads them to meaningful expression. We cannot teach students to do this; we can only facilitate their engagement with the process. A discussion with one of my administrators comes to my mind in the context of this point. The essence of their comment was: You are not a good teacher because you get strong students to do good work. You are a good teacher because you get struggling students to truly engage and produce good work. I had never thought about it from that perspective before, but I believe our acknowledgement of these important issues in art education finds clarity and value within the threshold concepts theoretical framework. The following chapter provides an in-depth introduction to the framework and its relevant constructs with the intention of providing a conceptual clarity of the case studies in the following chapters.

References

Aikenhead, G. S., & Elliott, D. (2010). An emerging decolonizing science education in Canada. *Canadian Journal of Science, Mathematics and Technology Education*, 10(4), 321–338.

Aubert, M., et al. (2014). Pleistocene cave art from Sulawesi, Indonesia. *Nature, 514*(7521), 223–226.

Bal, M. (2003). Visual essentialism and the object of visual culture. *Journal of Visual Culture, 2*(1), 5–32.

Barkan, M. (1955). *A foundation for art education.* Ronald Press.

Berliner, D. C. (2009, June). *Rational response to high-stakes testing and the special case of narrowing the curriculu* [Paper presentation]. The international conference on redesigning pedagogy. National Institute of Education, Nanyang Technological University, Singapore.

Blankstein, A. M., Noguera, P., & Kelly, L. (2016). *Excellence through equity: Five principles of courageous leadership to guide achievement for every student.* ASCD.

Brandt, P. A. (2004). *What is semiotics? The briefest overview ever seen.* https://sociosemiotics.net/files/whatissemiotics.pdf

Burton, J. M. (2009). Creative intelligence, creative practice: Lowenfeld redux. *Studies in Art Education, 50*(4), 323–337.

Chalmers, F. G. (2004). Learning from histories of art education: An overview of research and issues. In E. W. Eisner & M. D. Day (Eds.), *Handbook of research and policy in art education* (pp. 19–40). Routledge.

Chaplin, E. (2002). *Sociology and visual representation.* Routledge.

Debes, J. L. (1969). The loom of visual literacy – An overview. *Audiovisual Instruction, 14*(8), 25–27.

De Saussure, F. (1959). *Course in general linguistics.* Philosophical Library.

Dewey, J. (1916). *Democracy and education: An introduction to the philosophy of education.* Macmillan.

Dewey, J. (1934). *Art as experience.* Putnam.

Duncum, P. (2001). Visual culture: Developments, definitions, and directions for art education. *Studies in Art Education, 42*(2), 101–112.

Efland, A. D. (2017). *A history of art education.* Teachers College Press.

Eisner, E. W. (1972). *Educating artistic vision.* Macmillan.

Eisner, E. W. (1979). *The educational imagination: On the design and evaluation of school programs.* Macmillan.

Eisner, E. W. (1984). Alternative approaches to curriculum development in art education. *Studies in Art Education, 25*(4), 259–264.

Eisner, E. W. (Ed.). (1985). *Learning and teaching the ways of knowing.* University of Chicago Press.

Eisner, E. W. (2001). Should we create new aims for art education? *Art Education, 54*(5), 6–10.

Eisner, E. (2008). Art and knowledge. In J. G. Knowles & A. L. Cole (Eds.), *Handbook of the arts in qualitative research: Perspectives, methodologies, examples, and issues* (pp. 3–12). Sage.

Eisner, E. W., & Day, M. D. (Eds.). (2004). *Handbook of research and policy in art education*. Routledge.

England, K. V. (1994). Getting personal: Reflexivity, positionality, and feminist research. *Professional Geographer*, *46*(1), 80–89.

Fullan, M., & Boyle, A. (2014). *Big-city school reforms: Lessons from New York, Toronto, and London*. Teachers College Press.

Gay, G. (2010). *Culturally responsive teaching: Theory, research, and practice*. Teachers College Press.

Glassman, M. (2001). Dewey and Vygotsky: Society, experience, and inquiry in educational practice. *Educational Researcher*, *30*(4), 3–14.

Gude, O. (2004). Postmodern principles: In search of a 21st century art education. *Art Education*, *57*(1), 6–14.

Halagao, P. E. (2010). Liberating Filipino Americans through decolonizing curriculum. *Race, Ethnicity and Education*, *13*(4), 495–512.

Harnden, B., Rosales, A. B., & Greenfield, B. (2004). Outpatient art therapy with a suicidal adolescent female. *The Arts in Psychotherapy*, *31*(3), 165–180.

Heilig, J. V., Cole, H., & Aguilar, A. (2010). From Dewey to No Child Left Behind: The evolution and devolution of public arts education. *Arts Education Policy Review*, *111*(4), 136–145.

Henderson, K. (1999). *On line and on paper: Visual representations, visual culture, and computer graphics in design engineering*. MIT Press.

Hope, S. (2004). Art education in a world of cross-purposes. In E. W. Eisner & M. D. Day (Eds.), *Handbook of research and policy in art education* (pp. 93–112). Routledge.

Howard, G. R. (2016). *We can't teach what we don't know: White teachers, multiracial schools*. Teachers College Press.

Jones-Kavalier, B. R., & Flannigan, S. L. (2006). Connecting the digital dots: Literacy of the 21st century. *Educause Quarterly*, *29*(2), 8–10.

Knight, W. B. (2006). E(raced) bodies in and out of sight/cite/site. *Journal of Social Theory in Art Education*, *26*(1), 323–345.

Land, R., Rattray, J., & Vivian, P. (2014). Learning in the liminal space: A semiotic approach to threshold concepts. *Higher Education*, *67*(2), 199–217.

Leavy, P. (2009). *Method meets art: Arts-based research practice*. Guilford Press.

Leavy, P. (2015). *Method meets art: Arts-based research practice* (2nd ed.). Guilford Press.

Lowenfeld, V. (1947). Creative and mental growth: A textbook on art education. Macmillan.

Marling, K. A. (1994). *As seen on TV: The visual culture of everyday life in the 1950s*. Harvard University Press.

May, W. T. (1993). Teaching as a work of art in the medium of curriculum. *Theory into Practice*, *32*(4), 210–218.

Mirzoeff, N. (Ed.). (2002). *The visual culture reader*. Psychology Press.

Morgan, D. (1999). *Protestants and pictures: Religion, visual culture, and the age of American mass production.* Oxford University Press.

Ravenstahl, M. (2018). *Bringing the apple and holding up the mirror – A qualitative study of student engagement in visual art and the navigation of liminal space and transformation* [Unpublished PhD thesis]. Durham University.

Read, H. E. (1943). *Education through art.* Faber & Faber.

Sahlberg, P. (2011). *Finnish lessons.* Teachers College Press.

Smith-Shank, D. L. (1995). Semiotic pedagogy and art education. *Studies in Art Education, 36*(4), 233–241.

Wilson, B. (2000, May 17). *Of diagrams and rhizomes: Disrupting the content of art education* [Paper presentation]. The symposium of art education and visual culture at the Taipei Municipal Teachers College, Taipei, Taiwan.

Yenawine, P. (1997). Thoughts on visual literacy. In J. Flood, S. B. Heath, & D. Lapp (Eds.), *Handbook of research on teaching literacy through the communicative and visual arts* (pp. 845–860). Laurence Erlbaum.

Yenawine, P. (2003). Jump starting visual literacy: Thoughts on image selection. *Art Education, 56*(1), 6–12.

CHAPTER 3

Threshold Concepts

1   Threshold Crossing and Characteristics of Threshold Concepts

The origins of threshold concepts research began with Jan Meyer and Ray Land's participation in a United Kingdom research project focused on strong teaching and learning environments in the field of economics for undergraduates. The important observation resulting from their research was that "certain concepts were held by economists to be central to the mastery of their subject" (Cousin, 2006, p. 4) and from this notion the threshold concepts framework evolved. Meyer and Land (2006, p. 3) describe a threshold concept as a conceptual portal "opening up new and previously inaccessible ways of thinking about something." Implicit in this description is the aspect of transformation without which a learner cannot progress (Meyer & Land 2006). The inability of a learner to progress is characterized as them being in a "stuck place" (Ellsworth, 1989, 1997; Meyer & Land, 2005), where their attempt to understand is unable to progress. Individuals who are in a stuck place are also experiencing the liminal state which Meyer and Land (2006, p. 19) describe as integral to the crossing of thresholds: "passage through a portal or space that needs to be approached and negotiated" and "perhaps experienced as a transition in terms of sense of self." The liminal state is often troublesome and involves the affective dimension with unpleasant feelings and discomfort (the next section will delve deeper into understanding this complex state). The case studies presented in the next four chapters hold at its core the idea of the stuck place and liminality in conjunction with the transformative aspect of crossing conceptual portals, or thresholds. This interweaving of constructs (as they apply in threshold crossing) is where the epistemic elements of the art-making process can function as a semiotic vehicle empowering students to access knowledge and navigate affective elements associated with troublesome knowledge and their liminal experience (Ravenstahl, 2018; Ravenstahl & Rattray, 2019). In other words, in order to cross a threshold, it must be approached and its associated liminal experience navigated. It is an assumption that language or linguistic knowledge is the only means for knowledge construction that is relevant to threshold crossing and the navigation of liminal space. I argue that there are situations where the art-making process can facilitate the ability to cross thresholds and to undergo a transformative experience. The case studies presented in the following chapters document this liminal journey and threshold crossing within the student's artwork, writing, and interviews. It is important for me to be explicit that in writing this book I have had no interest in identifying specific threshold concepts unique to visual art. Instead, this book presents case studies where the art-making process provides valuable insight into the subjective experience of threshold crossing that was facilitated and documented within the art-making process.

Land, Meyer, and Baillie (2010) describe the crossing of thresholds as a journey where one must leave the familiar and relative safety and move into the unknown and potentially dangerous. Schwartzman (2010) adds that learning requires us to step into the unknown and results in a rupture of knowledge. It is essential that we understand the nature of threshold concepts and the nature of the difficulty of threshold crossing as it involves both the affective and cognitive dimensions. In other words, when individuals cross thresholds they undergo a transformed perception of self, worldview, or understanding of a subject landscape (Meyer & Land, 2006). The transformative characteristic of threshold concepts is an ontological and conceptual shift in knowledge that becomes a part of our perception and understanding of self (Cousin, 2006). The concept of transformative learning is discussed with greater depth later in this chapter but for establishing a basis for understanding threshold crossing it is imperative to highlight the non-negotiable element of transformation (Land, 2014; Schwartzman, 2010; Timmermans & Meyer, 2019).

Threshold concepts can often be mistaken for core concepts that are building blocks for a curriculum and important for a student to grasp in order to achieve success in a course. It is essential to make clear, however, that there is an important distinction between progressing through a curriculum and accessing knowledge or understanding that we previously were incapable of accessing. A more simplified understanding of this important distinction might be found in imagining core concepts as gathering bricks in a wheelbarrow for the building of something. We push the wheelbarrow around collecting bricks and we eventually fill the entire wheelbarrow. We can look around the yard and see progress in a sense. The wheelbarrow is full and tracks document our movement. We have clearly progressed and are prepared. Core concepts in our curriculum are the bricks that we master or comprehend that assist us in successfully progressing through a course, but what we do with these bricks outside of the context of the course is not quite known. Our perception has not changed regarding the world around us as a result of the successful completion of course material. Obviously, an appropriate metaphor for a threshold concept is a doorway that we approach and cross through (crawl, drive, sail, limp, claw, etc.). The important point in this metaphor is that we cross through a threshold into a new space where we perceive things differently than we had previously. When you enter a new space, you can look back through to the old space, but your understanding and sense of self is transformed. With core concepts you look back at the ground you covered and try to carry important concepts with you. When you cross a threshold your ontology (state of being), including thoughts, perceptions, and feelings, are inherent in how you experience and understand the environment around you, no matter where your journey leads.

The recent volume *Threshold Concepts in Practice* (Land et al., 2016) addresses threshold concepts from the much needed perspective of the student experience (Felten, 2016). Within this volume there is an important discussion of the affective element of threshold concepts (Rattray, 2016) and the construct of liminality. The point I am making here is that the crossing of thresholds and liminality is an internal experience that is unique to each individual and requires sensitivity on our part, as educators, to understand the complexity of the student's ontological state. The complexity of the affective dimension in the liminal experience is discussed with more depth later in this chapter. But for now, what matters is to establish that threshold crossing and liminality are complex and difficult states which reinforces the earlier notions that learning requires a risk and uncertainty. Therefore, we, as educators, must be able to establish emotional safety in our learning environments in order to empower students toward the brave space of engaging with liminality and becoming vulnerable in the process of transformation.

Meyer and Land (2006) identify characteristics of threshold concepts as being transformative, irreversible, integrative, troublesome, and bounded. Within this book the constructs of transformative, troublesome, and bounded are of relevance, as well as the discursive nature of threshold concepts. I will briefly introduce bounded and troublesome (as I did with transformative previously) and there will be more in-depth discussion of each of these constructs, later in the chapter.

Rourke and O'Connor (2013) conceptualize the construct of boundedness within the context of art and design. According to Rourke and O'Connor (2013), disciplines have borders and we can cross these conceptual borders, which can lead to developments in ourselves and, in turn, assist in the definition of the boundaries of a subject area. For the purposes of this book I am not interested in defining conceptual boundaries, but I am interested in the ability of visual art to cross boundaries, or act as a boundary object, that results in a transformed worldview. The issue of boundedness is important in the context of the visual arts. One of the underpinning reasons I have taken several chapters to describe and establish links between art education, the art-making process, and semiotic theory is due to the issue of boundedness. How do we know art making can transcend the limitations of the boundaries of art as a domain and express or construct meaning about ourselves or, for example, social issues? It is important that we, as educators, understand how this does occur and how we may facilitate this ability in all our students. In other words, the issue of boundedness is at the core of the art-making process having epistemic potential. This informs the observation that education in the arts is not and should not be limited to knowledge and mastery of skill that is contained within the field of visual art. By understanding the concept of boundedness, we, as educators, can feel empowered that our students can construct and express meaning that transcends the boundaries of art skill and design and informs transformation.

The construct of troublesome knowledge is often attributed to Perkins (1999) who states that troublesome knowledge is conceptually difficult, counterintuitive, alien, or incoherent. Meyer and Land (2003, p. 9) state that "the notion of threshold concepts might remain merely an interesting issue of cognitive organization" and perspective "if it were not for the consistent evidence of threshold concepts being troublesome." The relevance of this point is not only to provide some basic definition of the construct but to highlight the distinction between threshold crossing being a purely cognitive experience and the presumed association of troublesome knowledge to an affective dimension and a felt experience, which can point to the potential value of the art-making process.

Perkins (1999) identifies specific types of troublesome knowledge (including inert, conceptually difficult, and alien) but acknowledges there may be other sources of troublesomeness in knowledge. Meyer and Land (2006, p. 12) identify a type of tacit knowledge which is derived from the work of Polyani (1958) and is described as knowledge that "remains mainly personal and implicit." Meyer and Land (2006, p. 12) further conceptualize the construct of tacit knowledge by citing Giddens's (1984) description of "practical consciousness" as emergent and unexamined understandings. In other words, tacit knowledge is difficult to make explicit to other individuals although we possess and employ this knowledge (i.e., playing a musical instrument, creating an artwork). In this book, troublesome knowledge is conceptualized primarily as being tacit and ontological, which holds an arguably inherent and relevant interrelationship to visual art as well.

2   Liminality

The construct of the liminal space holds great significance in the threshold concepts framework and is central to this book and the presented case studies. The liminal state is an integral part of threshold crossing and could be described as a state of being that is difficult, unpleasant, disorienting, or challenging. Therefore, the liminal space is not a tangible or quantifiable measurement. Rather, the liminal state is experienced internally by the student and has affective involvement but with the awareness suggested in semiotic pedagogy we, as educators, can observe students experiencing the liminal state. When in the liminal space the student only has partial understanding of the respective threshold concept. It is important to remember that threshold crossing may involve academic contexts where a student is struggling to grasp concepts that change an understanding of a field of study. Or, relevant to this book, threshold crossing can also refer to complex and emotional changes in worldview and sense of self. Both involve unpleasant and uncomfortable states of being, but I would argue that some thresholds may be more complex or thorny than others, which is a common element in the case studies I present. The point is that I believe descriptions of threshold crossing and the liminal state suffer from the limitations of language. In my experience with the students whose experience I discuss in this book, there was profound emotional difficulty which was more effectively understood through their artistic journey than any linguistic description could ever provide. What can make an understanding of the liminal space even more confusing is that it can be experienced as a student is approaching or navigating the crossing of a threshold and it can also be experienced as a student transforms as a result of crossing a threshold. The feeling or affective involvement that is a part of the liminal experiences can have positive and negative implications. On the one hand, the liminal state is difficult, but it can motivate the learner to be productive and experimental in order to reduce the unpleasant feelings (Land, 2014). On the other hand, if the liminal experience is too profoundly difficult, a student may find engaging too challenging and overwhelming, and thereby not develop the ability to move forward. For example, someone who suffers from trauma may never be able to cope with the emotional troublesomeness of the liminal space. In addition, there is no specific amount of time or a pathway for navigating the liminal state. Therefore, someone may remain in a stuck place for periods of time and then find the ability to engage and progress while also progressing and regressing along the way.

The threshold literature often describes the liminal space as a transformative state or a "liquid space with great potential for learning, experimentation and growth" (Felten, 2016, p. 5). More specifically, the impact of the affective dimension on the ontological state can open the learner to try new means of knowledge construction or means of navigating the liminal space, which is a form of experimentation. The implication, in the context of my research, highlights the value of the art-making process and the inherent epistemological aspects. The exceptional individual may continue to search or experiment for ways to reduce unpleasant feelings, but in my experience most individuals (and especially high school students) are more likely to repeat and embrace familiar approaches to a point of frustration (Land, 2014). I argue that highly effective pedagogy in the twenty-first century exposes or introduces students to differing vehicles for understanding and it is this point that I believe the art-making process can reestablish true value in the education process. In my experience as an artist, educator, and researcher, there is unlimited potential in employing the inherent epistemic elements of the art-making process when students have access to this lens of understanding. Some of this experience is described in the case studies presented in later chapters.

Meyer and Land (2003, p. 21) describe liminality as "discursive and reconstitutive." As previously discussed, the liminal experience is associated with the transformative characteristic of crossing thresholds; the learner will demonstrate ontological shifts or changes in subjectivity. As educators, a primary indicator of the reconstitutive and transformative aspects is the enhanced language of learners that may be more sophisticated or more capable of articulating previously inaccessible thoughts and feelings. That the elements are intertwined to an extent in the reconstitutive (change in subjectivity) is often evidenced in the enhanced language of the learner. More simply put, when students experience these subjective changes, they develop the ability to put words to their feelings or experiences. I argue that visual language is an important aspect of this transformation and the discursive aspect of the art-making process holds a significant role.

Another aspect of these "transitionary states" (Meyer & Land, 2006, p. 22) is they act as rites of passage into communities of practice (Meyer & Land, 2005) in some disciplines. Thus far, I have tried to be explicit that the student's negotiation of liminality is neither limited to their rite of passage into the discipline of art or artist nor bounded to the domain of art and art education. The relationship of liminality and visual art focuses upon a negotiation of identity and sense of self. However, this is not to say that the students do not evolve as artists or cross thresholds related to this community of practice and domain. Although the focus of this book is to consider visual art as a semiotic vehicle for the navigation of liminality, the students represented in the case studies do become better artists. This is a secondary point (as strange as that seems), but in my experience the genuine engagement with epistemic aspects of art making empowers the crossing of conceptual boundaries as well as entry to a community of practice through a sophisticated understanding of the creative process.

THRESHOLD CONCEPTS

The issue of the vehicle employed to navigate liminality becomes more poignant when considering that learners may move back and forth across the liminal state. One may presume that the liminal state is straightforward or linear, but an individual may not traverse the liminal state in a straightforward manner. The navigation of the liminal space can be impacted by the affective and cognitive dimensions and the most effective vehicle may not be immediately associated with a domain. In this book, this issue relates back to the discursive element of threshold crossing, which was previously described as evidence of enhanced language. The original conceptualization presumes that language manifests as linguistic signs, but visual art is a form of nonlinguistic knowledge (Langer, 1957). The forms, materials, and other inherent qualities of visual art construct and express meaning. These discursive elements and the inherent epistemic elements can arguably be understood as vehicles for traversing liminal space. I argue that traditional vehicles which are often considered evidence of learning may not provide adequate means for negotiating liminal states that may be complex or thorny. The liminal state may be suspended due to a "lack of vehicle through which to express and progress his thinking" (Meyer & Land, 2006, p. 25).

Meyer and Land (2006) argue the subjective nature of thresholds and liminal experience which implies the complexity of the nature of the vehicle employed for traversing the liminal space. With this point in mind, I believe visual art making can act as a vehicle for the negotiation of liminality. In my experience, this aspect of visual art making is due to the subjectivity of the liminal experience along with affective elements that may require a means of engagement that is nonlinguistic.

3 Affective Dimension of Liminal Space and Art as a Vehicle for Navigation

My introduction of threshold concepts attempts to provide an explanation of what they are along with some understanding of their troublesome nature. Furthermore, I hope to elucidate the difficulty involved in threshold crossing, which involves a complex interrelationship between the cognitive and affective dimensions (Rattray, 2016). Due to this complex interrelationship, I believe visual art finds some relevance as a semiotic vehicle.

According to Rattray (2016),

> Threshold transformations foster ontological shifts that are associated with both cognitive and affective changes in the individual. They cause

> the individual to view and experience the world differently in terms, not just of the intellectual understanding of an idea but also in the way they feel about, or experience, the world. (p. 67)

The implicit point considers the extent to which liminality might be experienced as both a cognitive and affective state which is navigated by some students more easily than others (Rattray, 2016). Rattray's observation raises a salient point and interesting questions that open a door of relevance for research in the domain of the visual arts within the threshold literature. Does variation in the ability to navigate liminality have to do with individual attributes? In other words, some students may be more capable of navigating liminality than others due to their psychological capital (Rattray, 2016; Luthans & Youssef, 2004; Luthans et al., 2007). Rattray (2016) explores constructs of hope, optimism, emotional security, and resilience particularly as they pertain to psychological capital as a means of understanding variations in the willingness of individuals to engage with troublesomeness. The implication, on the one hand, is that personal psychological attributes can empower us to be more able to engage with troublesome experiences and feelings associated with liminality. On the other hand, some individuals may lack psychological attributes and psychological capital and can become overwhelmed or incapable of engaging with the complex affective elements that are associated with the liminal experience (Land, 2014) – for example, the death of a loved one or the struggle to be sober. Differing individuals may possess certain psychological capital and attributes that facilitate their ability to engage and navigate these troublesome experiences, allowing them to cross relevant thresholds and undergo transformations. Based on my experience as an art educator, I argue that the issue of the epistemic vehicle is another important consideration regarding students' engagement with powerful affective elements.

Within the positive psychology literature Reynolds and Lim (2007) research women with a diagnosis of cancer who turn to involvement with visual art making as a means of managing emotional distress and turmoil, filling occupational voids and regaining a sense of achievement and purpose. Reynolds and Lim (2007) conceptualize the diagnosis of cancer and ensuing impact upon the affective experiences of the respective patients as a form of post-traumatic stress and the study explores the patients turning to visual art to remediate this.

In a similar manner, Mathieson and Stam (1995) uses narrative as a means to explore identity work, which they define as "used to describe the process of patients' evaluations of the meaning of their illness within the actual context of ongoing, organized social relationships, including the medical system."

The study presents patients who use narrative to "make sense of their illness" and social relationships with the individual with a new identity of being ill (Mathieson & Stam, 1995, p. 283).

There are obvious distinctions that can be made between narrative and visual art, but the implicit association is the use of a creative process to make meaning of troublesome experiences and engage in reconstitutive aspects of thresholds. In these examples, there is clear involvement of the affective dimension which is obviously quite profound. The women struggling with cancer obviously experience powerful emotions about themselves, their families, and many other aspects of their lives. However, the threshold concept with which they grapple is to accept themselves as a sick person. The women come to terms with their new identity and sense of self that includes a terrible illness. Obviously, the art-making process does not cure or heal these women, but it did help some women to navigate a liminal state that involved powerful affective experiences. The crucial point is that the involvement of the affective dimension can be to such a degree that individuals may not be able to progress through the liminal space (Land, 2014). In this process the visual art-making process functioned as a vehicle to help the women come to terms with their sense of self as an individual with an illness.

This raises the question: Does the discipline or media employed as a vehicle impact the ability to engage the affective dimension and foster the navigation of liminality? Land (2014) argues that, on the one hand, the liminal experience with profound affective elements may cause individuals to repeat familiar but ineffective strategies to change their unpleasant state. On the other hand, the liminal state was previously described as a liquid state that can involve great experimentation (Meyer & Land, 2005; Felten, 2016). The domain of art (visual or narrative) seems to provide an epistemic vehicle for the individuals (in the studies) to construct meaning or engage with troublesomeness. The point being made is that creating visual art – being involved in a creative process – offers a unique means of engaging profound emotions, particularly in complex life experiences.

In the research by Reynolds and Lim (2007) and Mathieson and Stam (1995), the patients knowingly pursued a means to address or engage the ensuing emotions of a traumatic experience. In the context of the classroom, students do not knowingly enroll in an art class with this same intention. In my experience, students can employ the visual art-making process for powerful learning whether they planned on it or not. The case studies presented in this book employ the visual art-making process to engage very troubling experiences and feelings in a very organic manner. In other words, the epistemic function of the art-making process was not preconceived and only became incrementally clear to the students as they progressed through the liminal journey and as discursive characteristics of threshold crossing became apparent. The issues being raised about pedagogy and learning environments (throughout the first chapters) become increasingly relevant. The next section will discuss issues related to the affective dimension in the learning environment.

4 The Involvement of the Affective Dimension and Liminality in Learning Environments

In the context of the art-learning environment, the semiotic aspect of the art-making process can be a means to glimpse relevant thresholds and facilitate the navigation of the liminal space. Felten (2016) states a need for the threshold literature to address the student perspective in the learning process. I believe that art educators understanding the epistemic nature of the art-making process can allow us to facilitate student engagement with troublesome knowledge and experience. Whether this engagement is domain specific or beyond the school curriculum, liminality needs to be at the core of the student experience regarding learning. Learning requires a rupture of knowledge and varying degrees of discomfort (Schwartzman, 2010).

I think it is important to provide a substantive understanding of how threshold concepts, liminality, and the affective dimension can link to the learning environment. I have offered a lot of criticism of prescribed teaching and over-prescribed learning environments without offering solutions to my criticisms. Part of the title of my doctoral dissertation was "Bringing the Apple and Holding Up the Mirror." The references in this title are to the apple of knowledge from the Garden of Eden and the idea of a pedagogy that fosters self-reflection in a profound manner. Both metaphors require the recipients to engage in risks that possess a danger of disrupting the self. In my mind, this is a direct reference to the need for art education and specifically for educators to challenge students to employ visual art making for engagement with feelings and experiences that results in the expression of meaning.

Thus far in this book, I have argued that some art-learning environments rely on domain-specific knowledge, such as the principles and elements of design. The resulting work for students, in these contexts, tends to be focused on aesthetics and the demonstration of technical skill. Furthermore, there seems to be a social contract that we believe this artwork is a form of genuine self-expression as opposed to mere exercises in design or skill. When we consider threshold concepts and the discussion on semiotic pedagogy, there is a clear theoretical basis for the art-making process having importance in the education process. When we consider this discussion on the affective dimension and the ability of visual art to assist in glimpsing relevant thresholds, we can challenge our students in powerful ways.

The role of the affective dimension in learning environments (in my experience) is often ignored or only considered in contexts that focus on learning difficulties that magnify in traditional classroom situations. Most often the classroom context focuses upon cognition that can facilitate the aforementioned "banking" method (Freire, 1970) of teaching. Bloom (1956) identifies the generally accepted understanding of cognition as mental processes required to assimilate knowledge or information. I argue the importance or significance of the cognitive and affective dimensions may not be as easily discernible or prioritized as common assumptions suggest. In other words, the affective dimension can be a way of knowing, a means of knowledge construction, as well as a means to understand other individuals and contexts.

It is important to highlight that pedagogical approaches can be a response to the assessments that are required by states and school districts. In the United States, Standard of Learning exams are standardized tests that drive much of the classroom activity based on their high-stakes impact and the amount of material that must be covered. Land (2016) offers a critique of the gradual shifts toward what he calls consumerist education. This shift is based on "certainty, clarity, straightforwardness and control" (Land, 2016, p. 16), which values data and test scores as a means of justifying a valuable learning experience. Land (2016) contrasts consumerist education with learning as transformation, which is described as inherently involving the affective dimension and liminality, promoting discomfort and less certainty.

In my experience, this element of the struggle is often misconstrued in classrooms. The personal struggle associated with transformation requires an internalization and application of knowledge and skills to relevant life experience that results in the making of meaning that is embraced (Mezirow, 2000; Land, 2016). This is not the same as learners struggling to complete the tasks in a heavy workload or to score well on assessments. The issue of consumerist and standardized education has direct consequences upon classrooms and the students' experience and understanding of education. For example, Pope (2001) presents the students' view of school as being nothing more than a line on a curriculum vitae that enables the next step in advancement (college, job, marriage).

As previously discussed, Land (2016) and Pope (2001) find that issues of engagement and struggle can be misconstrued in classrooms that focus solely on the pragmatic issues of education. In the context of art education, struggle must involve the affective dimension and engagement must involve the internal self. This is not to say that all artwork must be about the artist themselves, but the creation of the work must involve a holistic engagement that goes beyond formulaic products.

Thus far, I have argued that art education has a unique opportunity to employ the art-making process as a vehicle for students to engage personal, troublesome knowledge and navigate associated liminal space. To be explicit: I am arguing that it is essential that we, as art educators, move toward designing our learning environments around the understanding of the art-making process. However, it is important to point out that pushing or challenging students in such a manner is not something that can be overtly done. Therefore, consideration of the affective dimension in the learning environment is more than just challenging students to truly engage. This requires us to rethink our assessment tasks and the nature of how we can have them facilitate art as a vehicle as opposed to a list of instructions that generate prescribed visual results. More importantly, as implied with semiotic pedagogy, we need to establish environments that are emotionally safe. I would argue that a pervasive emotional safety functions as an important structure of a classroom that empowers students to truly express themselves and experiment. This touches upon issues of equity as well when considering the diversity of student populations. The point being made is that the nature of our assignments is essential to allowing students the space to make work that is personal and which involves success and failure. However, the ability to engage in such an authentic art-making process requires a learning environment that embraces the affective elements of the liminal state. In my experience, when students are given the opportunity to engage genuinely in a creative process, they value the opportunity and engage (with varying degrees of enthusiasm). It is from this point, as an educator, I must change my mindset from telling students what to do with their artwork (as they progress) to seeing an opportunity to read their work and allow the visual expression to inform questions and ensuing discourse. It is in this process that students begin to realize the potential and substance of their work by engaging in a dialogue that ignites an understanding of their perspectives and intentions. In cases where the work involves intimate and painful experiences, the artwork can function as a boundary object in the sense of discourse. In other words, the artwork can allow me (and other educators) the opportunity to ask questions through the visual elements of the artwork and, in turn, the student can respond or discuss more vulnerable experiences and feelings through the artwork.

These aspects of the art-learning environment allow for the affective dimension to become integrated and a part of our learning environments. In my experience, when this affective element is inherent and pervasive students begin to utilize the art-making process for authentic learning that leads to transformative experiences.

5   Transformative Theory

Transformative theory, according to Mezirow (2000, p. 3), is predicated upon the "urgent need to understand and order the meaning of our experience." Implicit in this concept is Piaget's notion of accommodation, which is when the organism changes itself to take in new influences from the surrounding environment (Piaget, 1976; Huitt & Hummel, 2003; Wadsworth, 1996; Illeris, 2007). This change is in order to maintain equilibrium and avoid a prolonged state of disequilibrium (Piaget, 1976; Illeris, 2007; Huitt & Hummel, 2003). Disequilibrium occurs when individuals engage in and with new experiences that conflict with their existing knowledge (Piaget, 1976; Huitt & Hummel, 2003; Wadsworth, 1996; Illeris, 2007). Transformative theory builds upon the assumption of the human need for understanding and making meaning of our experience and to integrate it with what we know. According to Mezirow (2000, p. 5), "learning is understood as the process of using a prior interpretation to construe a new or revised interpretation of the meaning of one's experience as a guide to future action." However, our revised interpretations are challenged by our habits of mind or sets of assumptions that influence our interpretations of experiences (Mezirow & Associates, 1990, p. 1). The implication that needs to be more explicit is the presence of the affective dimension and the complexity of the cognitive processes. In my view, these academic conceptualizations understate the complexity of the transformative process.

Transformative learning is "a deep, structural shift in basic premises of thought, feelings, and actions" (Transformative Learning Centre, 2004, cited in Kitchenham, 2008, p. 104). Mezirow (2000, p. 6) also argued that transformative learning is often "an intensely threatening emotional experience" due to our subjective challenge to our taken-for-granted frames of reference. There is an inherent affective element to transformative learning that makes an important distinction regarding the conceptualization of learning, so that the affective element in knowledge construction and engagement with experience becomes highly relevant and present within the learning process. Furthermore, this is indicative of conceptualizations of knowledge that, according to Perkins (1999), are troublesome, tacit, and ontological.

There are several facets to the relevance of transformative theory regarding this book and in my experience of understanding art education. As previously discussed, crossing thresholds possess a transformative quality that results in a shift in perception and understanding. The case studies presented in the next four chapters, in my view, present students who experienced personal transformations or ontological shifts. These students did not enter the art courses with the intention of engaging with profound life experiences and feelings and ultimately experiencing transformation. Nor did I present a lesson that asked students to make art about painful experiences. In my mind, the important point here is the way the learning environment is structured with consideration of the affective dimension and the semiotic aspects of the visual art-making process. I argue that in this emotional and psychological context the art-making process can become more than grades on assignments and a means to facilitate complex personal journeys that are wrought with emotion and difficulty. I chose to write about these students due to the obvious complexity of their stories and the organic way the art-making process facilitated their journey. It is important to be explicit in that neither I nor the students are making causal claims. In other words, I am not trying to argue that making art "fixed" anybody and neither do the students presented in the case studies. The important point is that the art-making process acted as a unique semiotic vehicle for students who had been struggling with making meaning out of their experiences. The art-making process played an important role as nonlinguistic knowledge construction and a means of navigating a liminal experience that is wrought with affective involvement. Each of the cases is a unique journey involving troublesome knowledge and life experiences and toward an ontological shift that is documented and empowered by the art-making process.

6 Troublesome, Tacit, and Ontological Knowledge and the Liminal State

Perkins provides a foundation for threshold concepts with his work addressing nuances of knowledge. Perkins (1999) identifies troublesome knowledge as knowledge that seems counterintuitive, foreign, or even intellectually absurd as an individual first engages with it. Presumably, troublesome knowledge holds a relationship to the construct of disequilibrium. This means troublesome knowledge does not align with an individual's existing knowledge. Moreover, Meyer and Land (2003) state that troublesomeness is a characteristic of the liminal state and the crossing of thresholds. The case studies in this book present troublesome knowledge as associated with past experiences, which continually impacted the students, who remained in a stuck place. More specifically, the students were unable to process the past experiences with its implicit affective and cognitive elements.

In this book, troublesomeness takes the form of tacit and ontological knowledge. Tacit knowledge is described by Meyer and Land (2003) as mainly personal and implicit and Polyani (1958) further describes it as a level of "practical consciousness." Giddens (1984, cited in Meyer & Land, 2006, p. 12) conceptualizes tacit knowledge as being "emergent but unexamined understandings."

THRESHOLD CONCEPTS 51

One may construe these meanings as a form of subconscious thought or knowledge yet to be engaged with on a more direct and conscious level of awareness. Ellsworth (1989, 1997) conceptualizes ontological knowledge as inherent knowledge that results from the unique experiences associated with race, religion, ethnicity, or economic, physical, or mental disadvantages that shape perception and understanding. One may simplify ontological knowledge as being implicit in one's being and inextricable from an individual's experiences. In the context of this study there are clear associations with the constructs of tacit and ontological knowledge which highlight the relevance of the visual art-making process as a means of learning or navigating the liminal state.

As formerly discussed, liminality was described as a space where individuals may become highly experimental and capable of ontological shifts (Meyer & Land, 2005; Felten, 2016). It can be argued the art-learning environment and the art-making process may be well suited for fostering these qualities of liminality. In my experience and as presented in the case studies, the student's work became more compelling as a visual experience and expressed a meaning that can be perceived by others in the interpretation of symbols and manipulation of materials. These observations present evidence of the student being in the liminal state and the artwork is a physical form of representation of the student's attempt to navigate liminality.

The point being made here is to highlight that relationships between threshold concepts and art education do not devalue or de-emphasize the importance of the visual experience of the artwork. In my experience, the students become better artists because they have been able to give physical representation to a genuine and authentic voice. The residual feelings of the troublesome knowledge and liminal space can be engaged with in powerful ways through the art-making process.

7 Visual Art as Insight into the Experience of the Liminal State

> What makes material a medium is that it is used to express a meaning which is other than that which it is in virtue of its bare physical existence. (Dewey, 1934, p. 201)

The strongest evidence of the ability of visual art to give form to the liminal state is found in the domain of art therapy. Sibbett and Thompson (2008) predicate their research upon the inherent relationship of the liminal state and what Turner (1995, p. 128) calls, "an urge to generate 'symbols, rituals [...] and works of art.'" Sibbett and Thompson (2008, p. 230) further argue that it is essential to effectively utilize the "reflexive symbolic and art expression generated by liminality as a means of navigating it."

The argument being established is that there are domains where the art-making process has been utilized to engage with troublesome experiences. There is a long history of art fostering the ability for individuals to process trauma that involves complex affective and cognitive elements. Clearly, in the field of art therapy there is counseling and other components to assisting a patient, but art is a valuable tool in this process. Furthermore, there is an urgency to reduce the discomfort which is accompanied by a willingness to experiment and increased productivity (Land, 2014). In the context of the case studies the students discover this epistemic potential of art making in an organic manner. The ability to understand and utilize this potential of the art-making process was in part due to the learning environment and the nature of how I present the conceptual nature of the process. It is important to note that I do not attempt to perform therapy in my art courses, which is explained and made explicit in the discussion on ethics. However, the artwork does provide form to complex and troublesome experience which informs discussion between the students and me (and outside psychological help in some cases).

The previous discussion of art therapy is also relevant to issues of boundedness but the core point being made was to establish a theoretical context for art making to engage troublesome experience and complex cognitive and affective involvement. However, another important element to the visual art-making process to provide insight into the navigation of liminality is the art-based research literature. Eisner (1981; Denzin and Lincoln, 2008) argues that arts-based educational research (ABER) provides a kind of emotional and interpersonal description that allows for unique understanding within the social sciences that departs from the limitations of literal scientific description. In *Method Meets Art* (2009), Patricia Leavy argues that ABER practices offer researchers "new pathways for creating knowledge within and across disciplinary boundaries" (Leavy, 2009, p. IX). Furthermore, these practices are employed in all phases of research, including data collection, analysis, interpretation, and representation resulting in more "holistic and engaged ways in which theory and practice are intertwined" (ibid.).

I argue that this same understanding of the art-making process can be applied to students in the art studio environment and specifically for the case studies used in this book. Knowles and Thomas (2002, cited in Leavy, 2015) conducted a study that was a participatory arts-based method. The study focused upon a sense of place in school and upon the experience of school from the student's perspective. Knowles and Thomas (2002, cited in Leavy, 2015) highlight an example where a young woman drew a portrait that is cropped closely around her face. The young woman states this is representative of the lack of freedom she feels at school. My point in this example is the young woman may have been experiencing these feelings and the process of drawing moved these feelings from a tacit dimension to being articulated in visual and linguistic signs. In other words, the involvement in the study may have given her an opportunity to recognize her perspective and give it meaning, as opposed to having an opportunity to express something that was being stifled.

The ABER literature frequently conceptualizes the researcher as someone who can "merge their artist self with their scholar self" (Leavy, 2009, p. 2), which is further understood in the a/r/tography literature as the practitioner occupying an in-between space which merges knowing, doing, and making (Springgay et al., 2005). The relevance of understanding this point is understanding that the student is acting in a similar capacity. More specifically, the student is employing the art-making experience to engage with troublesomeness and navigate the liminal state by indulging the "urges" for expression and form. I am not arguing that the student is engaging in art therapy or ABER, but is drawing from the same epistemic characteristics. The art produced is tangible evidence of the liminal journey and offers insight into its subjective experience.

When considered in this manner, one may conclude that the role of the arts educator is to utilize the creative process as a means of leading students toward troublesomeness and the liminal state. Jaspers (1931, p. 716) discusses the revealing function of art and argues that "[a]rts-based expression and learning offers the potential for revelatory inclusion of that which otherwise might be excluded as taboo." In the context of the case studies in this book, there are strong correlations between the urges of liminality and the revelatory factors of the art-making process.

Implicit in the arguments made in this section are issues of boundedness and semiotic theory. The case studies in this book (as previously stated) exploit the epistemic potential of the visual art-making process. As the opening quote states the materials, their use become a medium that gives form to profound life experience. Furthermore, it fosters and provides insight into their complex liminal journey. Within the following sections there will be discussion on boundedness, semiotic theory, and the discursive aspects of threshold concepts. This discourse will provide further insight for the reader into the nature of visual art as a means of navigation of the liminal space.

8 Boundedness and Boundary Objects

Meyer and Land (2003) state an identifying characteristic of threshold concepts is the issue of their being bounded. More specifically, Meyer and Land (2003) acknowledge the reality of distinctions between academic disciplines and their conceptual frontiers. The issue of boundedness is central to this book as the focus of the art-making process engages life experience and meaning that falls outside the specific domain of art. However, the art-making process is essential to the knowledge construction and understandings that the young people ultimately derive. There is an interrelationship that involves the art-making process but transcends the domain of art. The issue of boundedness is highly relevant in the consideration of visual art as a means of navigating liminality, which is addressed to some degree in the previous sections. The students employ the elements and principles of art but formulate knowledge and meaning relevant to their own human development and well-being. I have also offered (earlier in this book) criticism that art education is often assumed to always result in critical thought and reflection. Therefore, there must be substantive discussion of boundedness in order to give credibility to my own claims about the art-making process.

Akkerman and Bakker (2011, p. 136) state boundary objects possess a "bridging function" which "refer to ongoing, two-sided actions and interactions between contexts. These actions and interactions across sites are argued to affect not only the individual but also the different social practices at large." Akkerman and Bakker (2011, p. 136) distinguish boundary crossing from transfer, which is "a unique instance in which something learned in a given context is applied to another context." I argue the artwork in this book functions as a form of boundary object. When considered as a conceptual subject the visual arts are bounded in that there is development specific to the field itself regarding use of material and form. But when considered in relationship to the liminal experience and the affective dimension there is meaning and expression of experience that transcends the subject of visual art. I argue it is these affective elements and troublesome experiences that provides substance for art making to transcend the boundaries of the domain of art. Wenger (1998, p. 58) argues that boundary objects are based on "reification," which is "the process of giving form to our experience by producing objects that congeal this experience into "thingness." Wenger's statement is indicative of the art-making process, as understood in the case studies. The transformative boundary objects in the literature (Akkerman & Bakker, 2011) are experienced as interpretive engagement with an externally existing object. In the case of visual art, we are considering an object that is born into existence from the internal cognitive and affective dimension, which provides a form of representation of the student's experiences. It would be obtuse to ignore the obvious and distinct differences of interpreting an object versus the complex processing of creating the object that makes tacit and ontological knowledge explicit and concrete. Upon further consideration, it can be argued that the art-making process acts as a form of "reification."

When the visual art-learning environment extends beyond the replication of technical exercise there is opportunity for student artwork to become boundary objects that cross conceptual frontiers. This book is predicated upon the notion of boundary and threshold crossing facilitated by the art-making process. Therefore, the issue of language becomes an inextricable element. The art-making process becomes a unique form of processing the experience of the affective dimension and evolving cognitive understanding; it can be argued that the art-making process provides a means of inner discourse through non-linguistic signs and signifiers.

9 Discursive Element and Visual Art: Linguistic and Nonlinguistic Knowledge and Self-Dialogue

The discursive element is described by Meyer and Land (2005) as a noted change in the sophistication or the enhanced use of language relevant to a respective community of practice. When a student traverses threshold concepts they are capable of discourse that is substantive and indicative of understanding that transcends their previous ontological state. The change in the discursive element of threshold concepts is representative of "a reconstitution of the learners' subjectivity" and results in "new and empowering forms of expression that in many instances characterize distinctive ways of disciplinary thinking" (Meyer & Land, 2006, pp. 20–21). In the context of this book and visual art, the discursive element is more complex than has been described thus far, and further discussion can be framed as linguistic and nonlinguistic knowledge and self-dialogue.

Rudolf Arnheim (1954, 1966) and Susanne Langer (1942, 1953) emphasized cognitive aspects of the arts to large academic audiences and highlighted the intellectual basis for approaching art making as serious inquiry (McNiff, 2008). As a result, the domain of art-based research is a more focused application of the larger epistemological process of artistic knowing and inquiry. Moreover, arts-based research is an extension of a significant increase of studies researching the nature of the art experience in higher education and professional practice (McNiff, 1998). I am contextualizing the case studies in the following chapters within this discussion. My justification for doing so is the extension of the epistemological process of the art experience in certain situations in secondary learning environments. In my experience, students arguably cross a threshold and experience transformation that the art process facilitated to some degree. This raises the argument of the nature of the discursive element in the context of visual art as a facilitation to threshold crossing. More specifically, Meyer and Land (2005) clearly presume linguistic knowledge as an indicator of enhanced language as a result of transformation. However, in the case studies presented there is a change in the sophistication of the visual work that becomes much more expressive of complex experience. I argue this visual language is also evidence of the discursive element of threshold crossing.

The epistemic core of ABER is a distinction of different forms of knowing; the literature "distinguishes between discursive and nondiscursive modes of knowing" (Langer, 1957, cited in Barone & Eisner, 2012, p. 9). More specifically, the distinction is that ABER is an emotional expression (as opposed to a description) with the intention of understanding how others feel, by using different forms of representation (Barone & Eisner, 2012). When considered in this manner, one may construe, the presented cases are engaging in a manner of merging the scholar and the artistic self (Leavy, 2009). An implication suggests the role the of arts educator is to utilize the creative process as a means of leading students toward troublesome knowledge and ultimately the liminal state. As stated by Perkins (1999, p. 5): "Qualitative problems lead students to confront the character of the phenomenon rather than master computational routines."

Another implication of the art-making process as nonlinguistic knowledge is the internal and possibly tacit nature of knowledge construction. In the thresholds literature there are many claims to alternative or nondiscursive forms of dialogue (Arnheim, 1954, 1966; Langer, 1942, 1953). Obviously, within this context, the artwork acts as a form of "cultural practice" (Bhabha, 1990) that engages with and expresses experiences to others. However, in this installation the issue of dialogue is not as relevant to the media in which it transpires but the fact it is a dialogue with the self or, as Marková (2006) states, the ego. In my experience, students can engage in a dialogue with the self that is internal and can involve the complexity of the affective dimension. Others eventually have access to the student's artwork and can derive meaning from it, but the student's experience is one of dialogue with the self or a form of reflection that engages feeling and experience.

Chi et al. (1989) state that self-explaining is a means of knowledge construction that has had impact in academic classrooms. Meyer and Land (2006) clarify that self-explanation theory requires an "awareness of changing understanding" and when considered in conjunction with different forms of representation, highlights the potential for research into the "dynamics involved in reaching understanding" (Meyer & Land, 2006, p. 65). It can be argued that the students employ the visual art process as a means of self-dialogue or self-explanation. Especially when the evidence of a transformed worldview is considered, it is clear the art-making process played a role in the affective and cognitive changes regarding the cases discussed in this book. However, as previously stated, there are many experiences that stimulated the troublesome knowledge and potential liminality that, in turn, may have assisted in a growth process. Therefore, it suggests the relevance of claims toward the epistemic role of the visual art-making process regarding this transformation and the integral role of the affective dimension.

10   Conclusion

This chapter was meant to clarify and conceptualize the meaning of threshold concepts and the relevant associated constructs. More importantly, it establishes clear and substantive interrelationships between threshold concepts, semiotic pedagogy, and the importance of the affective dimension. The point of this interrelationship is not only to make them explicit but to establish how they create an effective lens to understand the potential of art-learning environments and the art-making process in the twenty-first century.

The following four chapters present case studies of four students whom I have taught and received permission from to use their stories and artworks for this book. The case studies each present a student that used the art-making process to navigate and potentially cross thresholds related to aspects of self and identity. These students were selected in part because the liminal journey is a powerful story that is navigated through the art-making process. Therefore, the artwork acts as a documentation of their liminal experience and it was through the artwork that both the students and I could give voice to the issues with which the students struggled. The selection of the students was done organically and was not performed as a predetermined experimental research but as a documentation of their journeys that has shed light on the value of art education and the importance of art educators to understand the more conceptual aspects of art making along with the nature of our learning environments.

The case studies present the personal stories of the students in varying detail. The case studies also present art portfolios and sketchbook pages from the students. The art portfolios consist of artwork selected by the respective students to submit for final external assessment for the curriculum our school offers. The relevance of making this explicit is to ensure that our classroom interactions were always focused upon the development of the student work in a manner that was organic and natural to their artistic vision and language. The idea to include them in this book came at a time after the students had already graduated. Therefore, the artwork presented and the ideas expressed were collected at a time before the writing of this book. In addition to the art portfolios and sketchbooks pages, I conducted interviews with the students toward the end of their respective school years and after they had submitted their work for external assessment. The interviews are a form of reflection for the student upon their journey which offers insight into different aspects of their thinking and learning over the time we worked together.

References

Akkerman, S. F., & Bakker, A. (2011). Boundary crossing and boundary objects. *Review of Educational Research, 81*(2), 132–169.

Arnheim, R. (1954). *Art and visual perception.* University of California Press.

Arnheim, R. (1966). *Toward a psychology of art: Collected essays.* University of California Press.

Barone, T., & Eisner, E. W. (2012). What is and what is not arts based research? In T. Barone & E. W. Eisner (Eds.), *Arts based research* (pp. 1–12). Sage. https://www.doi.org/10.4135/9781452230627.n1

Bhabha, H. (1990). The third space: Interview with Homi Bhabha. In J. Rutherford (Ed.), *Identity: Community, culture, difference* (pp. 207–221). Lawrence & Wishart.

Bloom, B. S. (1956). *Taxonomy of educational objectives: The classification of educational goals.* Longman.

Chi, M. T., Bassok, M., Lewis, M. W., Reimann, P., & Glaser, R. (1989). Self-explanations: How students study and use examples in learning to solve problems. *Cognitive Science, 13*(2), 145–182.

Cousin, G. (2006). An introduction to threshold concepts. *Planet, 17*(1), 4–5. doi:10.11120/plan.2006.00170004

Denzin, N. K., & Lincoln, Y. S. (Eds.). (2008). *Collecting and interpreting qualitative materials* (3rd ed.). Sage.

Dewey, J. (1934). *Art as experience.* Putnam.

Eisner, E. W. (1981). On the differences between scientific and artistic approaches to qualitative research. *Educational Researcher, 10*(4), 5–9. https://doi.org/10.3102/0013189X010004005

Ellsworth, E. (1989). Why doesn't this feel empowering? Working through the repressive myths of critical pedagogy. *Harvard Educational Review, 59*(3), 297–325.

Ellsworth, E. (1997). *Teaching positions: Difference, pedagogy, and the power of address.* Teachers College Press.

Felten, P. (2016). Introduction: Crossing thresholds together. *Teaching and Learning Together in Higher Education, 1*(9). http://repository.brynmawr.edu/tlthe/vol1/iss9/1

Freire, P. (1970). *Pedagogy of the oppressed.* Seabury Press.

Giddens, A. (1984). *The constitution of society: Outline of the theory of structuration.* Polity.

Huitt, W., & Hummel, J. (2003). Piaget's theory of cognitive development. *Educational Psychology Interactive*, *3*(2), 1–5.

Illeris, K. (2007). *How we learn: Learning and non-learning in school and beyond.* Routledge.

Jaspers, K. (1931). *Die geistige Situation unserer Zeit.* Sammlung Göschen.

Kitchenham, A. (2008). The evolution of John Mezirow's transformative learning theory. *Journal of Transformative Education*, *6*(2), 104–123.

Knowles, J. G., & Thomas, S. (2002). Artistry, inquiry and sense-of-place. In C. Bagley & M. B. Cancienne (Eds.), *Dancing the data* (pp. 121–132). Peter Lang.

Land, R. (2014, July). *Liminality close-up* [Paper presentation]. HECU7 at Lancaster University.

Land, R. (2016). Toil and trouble: Threshold concepts as a pedagogy of uncertainty. In R. Land, J. H. F. Meyer, & M. T. Flanagan (Eds.), *Threshold concepts in practice* (pp. 11–24). Sense.

Land, R., Meyer, J. H. F., & Baillie, C. (2010). Editors' preface: Threshold concepts and transformational learning. In J. H. F. Meyer, R. Land, & C. Baillie (Eds.), *Threshold concepts and transformational learning* (pp. ix–xlii). Sense.

Land, R., Meyer, J. H. F., & Flanagan, M. T. (Eds.). (2016). *Threshold concepts in practice.* Sense.

Langer, S. K. (1942). *Philosophy in a new key: A study in the symbolism of reason, rite and art.* Harvard University Press.

Langer, S. K. (1953). *Feeling and form: A theory of art.* Scribner.

Langer, S. K. (1957). *Problems of art: Ten philosophical lectures.* Scribner.

Leavy, P. (2009). *Method meets art: Arts-based research practice.* Guilford Press.

Leavy, P. (2015). *Method meets art: Arts-based research practice* (2nd ed.). Guilford Press.

Luthans, F., & Youssef, C. M. (2004). Human, social, and now positive psychological capital management: Investing in people for competitive advantage. *Organizational Dynamics*, *33*(2), 143–160.

Luthans, F., Youssef, C. M., & Avolio, B. J. (2007). *Psychological capital.* Oxford University Press.

Marková, I. (2006). On the "inner alter" in dialogue. *International Journal for Dialogical Science*, *1*(1), 125–147.

Mathieson, C. M., & Stam, H. J. (1995). Renegotiating identity: Cancer narratives. *Sociology of Health & Illness*, *17*(3), 283–306.

McNiff, S. (1998). *Art-based research.* Jessica Kingsley Publishers.

McNiff, S. (2008). Art-based research. In J. G. Knowles & A. L. Cole (Eds.), *Handbook of the arts in qualitative research: Perspectives, methodologies, examples, and issues* (pp. 29–40). Sage.

Meyer, J. H. F., & Land, R. (2003). Threshold concepts and troublesome knowledge (1): Linkages to ways of thinking and practising within the disciplines. In C. Rust (Ed.), *Improving student learning theory and practice – Ten years on* (pp. 412–424). Oxford Centre for Staff & Learning Development.

Meyer, J. H. F., & Land, R. (2005). Threshold concepts and troublesome knowledge (2): Epistemological considerations and a conceptual framework for teaching and learning. *Higher Education, 49*(3), 373–388. https://doi.org/10.1007/s10734-004-6779-5

Meyer, J. H. F., & Land, R. (Eds.). (2006). *Overcoming barriers to student understanding: Threshold concepts and troublesome knowledge.* Routledge.

Mezirow, J. (1990). How critical reflection triggers transformative learning In J. Mezirow & Associates (Eds.), *Fostering critical reflection in adulthood: A guide to transformative and emancipatory learning.* Jossey-Bass Publishers.

Mezirow, J. (1991). *Transformative dimensions of adult learning.* Jossey-Bass.

Mezirow, J. (2000). Learning to think like an adult: Core concepts of transformation theory. In J. Mezirow & Associates (Eds.), *Learning as transformation: Critical perspectives on a theory in progress* (pp. 3–33). Jossey-Bass.

Perkins, D. (1999). The many faces of constructivism. *Educational Leadership, 57*(3), 6–11.

Piaget, J. (1976). Piaget's theory. In B. Inhelder & C. Zwingmann (Eds.), *Piaget and his school: A reader in developmental psychology* (pp. 11–23). Springer.

Polanyi, M. (1958). *The study of man.* University of Chicago Press.

Pope, D. C. (2001). *Doing school: How we are creating a generation of stressed out, materialistic, and miseducated students.* Yale University Press.

Rattray, J. (2016). Affective dimensions of liminality. In R. Land, J. H. F. Meyer, & M. T. Flanagan (Eds.), *Threshold concepts in practice* (pp. 67–76). Sense.

Ravenstahl, M. J. (2018). *Bringing the apple and holding up the mirror – A qualitative study of student engagement in visual art and the navigation of liminal space and transformation* [Unpublished PhD thesis]. Durham University.

Ravenstahl, M. J., & Rattray, J. (2019). Bringing the apple and holding up the mirror: Liminal space and transformation in visual art making. In J. A. Timmermans & R. Land (Eds.), *Threshold concepts on the edge* (pp. 127–142). Brill Sense.

Reynolds, F., & Lim, K. H. (2007). Turning to art as a positive way of living with cancer: A qualitative study of personal motives and contextual influences. *Journal of Positive Psychology, 2*(1), 66–75.

Rourke, A. J., & O'Connor, Z. (2013). Threshold concept: Overcoming the stumbling blocks to learning design history and colour theory in higher education. *Design Principles & Practice: An International Journal: Annual Review, 6*, 23–31.

Schwartzman, L. (2010). Transcending disciplinary boundaries: A proposed theoretical foundation for threshold concepts. In J. H. F. Meyer, R. Land, & C. Baillie (Eds.), *Threshold concepts and transformational learning* (pp. 21–44). Sense.

Sibbett, C., & Thompson, W. (2008). Nettlesome knowledge, liminality and the taboo in cancer and art therapy experiences: Implications for learning and teaching. In R. Land, J. H. F. Meyer, & J. Smith (Eds.), *Threshold concepts within the disciplines* (pp. 227–242). Brill.

Smith-Shank, D. L. (1995). Semiotic pedagogy and art education. *Studies in Art Education, 36*(4), 233–241.

Springgay, S., Irwin, R. L., & Kind, S. W. (2005). A/r/tography as living inquiry through art and text. *Qualitative Inquiry, 11*(6), 897–912.

The Transformative Learning Centre. (2004). The Transformative Learning Centre. Retrieved July 27, 2004, from http://tlc.oise.utoronto.ca/index.htm ransformative

Timmermans, J. A., & Meyer, J. H. (2019). A framework for working with university teachers to create and embed "Integrated Threshold Concept Knowledge" (ITCK) in their practice. *International Journal for Academic Development, 24*(4), 354–368.

Turner, V. (1995). *The ritual process: Structure and anti-structure.* Transaction Publishers.

Wadsworth, B. J. (1996). *Piaget's theory of cognitive and affective development: Foundations of constructivism* (5th ed.). Longman.

Wenger, E. (1998). *Communities of practice: Learning, meaning and identity.* Cambridge University Press.

CHAPTER 4

Jayden: A Split Self

1 Introduction

The young woman who is the focus of this case study is named Jayden. She experienced profound questions and uncertainty regarding her identity and an understanding of herself due to complex interrelationships of racial composition and socialization. Jayden was born to a white female and a black male, which had obvious genetic influence upon her physical features. Further complexity resides in the fact that Jayden was adopted by a white family which experienced dramatic life change soon after her adoption. Jayden's social context during early child-hood was upper class and she attended predominantly white private schools. Because of a dramatic change Jayden's social reality switched to urban public schools with a much more diverse demographic regarding race, ethnicity, and economic status. These differing social contexts placed Jayden in extremes of not only socioeconomic realities, but she formed bonds and relationships with peer groups of extremely different racial and economic backgrounds. A consequence of these extremes of social context raised questions within Jayden regarding her racial identity and, ultimately, her sense of self. In addition, Jayden was, with some frequency, confronted with comments, questions, and observations that in some cases were racist and hurtful, penetrating the affective dimension.

Jayden's understanding of identity is troublesome, and the liminal journey is plotted in this way. The artwork demonstrates an emotional and cognitive engagement with racial identity and stereotypes that moves internally to the core of Jayden. Moreover, the artwork documents an ontological shift where the visual representation of feelings and experiences is a semiotic navigation of the liminal space. In Jayden's experience, identity is a complex emotional threshold and visual semiotics guides Jayden through the liminal space; the art-making process facilitates her ability to talk about her complex journey through the thresholds of identity and self. In short, she uses visual signs and signifiers before linguistic ones.

2 Jayden

As the introduction presents, Jayden began her education at an "all-white private school" where she and one other child were the only individuals of color. "That

© KONINKLIJKE BRILL NV, LEIDEN, 2022 | DOI:10.1163/9789004508132_004

kind of shaped who I was. I was always very, I guess, white" (Jayden). Implicit in her description is the suggestion that her early childhood environment resulted in a socialization to be white. More specifically, Berger and Luckmann (1966, p. 152) state, "the self is a reflected entity" meaning that it is a "dialectic between identification by others and self-identification." Jayden states in the interviews that she always associated her own heritage as being the same as her mother's, even though she was adopted she did not make a distinction between her mother's ethnic heritage and her own. I argue Jayden identified through the emotional and psychological interactions with her mother, which allowed Jayden to disregard racial differences between her mother and herself.

Although socialization is not a focus of this book, it is a point at which troublesome knowledge finds origins. Jayden's experiences uncover a struggle with understanding and accepting her identity and sense of self due to the diverse racial experiences of her upbringing. More specifically, Jayden's early childhood was in an affluent white area and then, due to the death of her adoptive father, she moved to a more diverse area where she befriended other black adolescents. While Jayden does not have a problem being raised by a white family, the reality of being a black female has come into conflict with the social reality of being African American and the different racial assumptions made about her as a mixed-race person. "That's when, like, mass confusion set in" (Jayden). Her earliest memory of experiencing conflict in racial identity and self was in third grade. Jayden's class was assigned a book on Martin Luther King Jr., which she brought home and read.

> The very next day, I was, like, Mom. You're horrible. Your people did this to my people. I think that's when like the mass confusion started. Because I was like but, wait. I'm white, too. But I'm also black. It was, like, my people doing this to my people. There was just like a huge conflict that I couldn't handle [it], especially at such a young age. (Jayden)

I asked Jayden if that was the earliest she could remember a conflict in racial identity, and she affirmed this was the first moment; her appearance and internal identification were in direct conflict. The interviews with Jayden reveal a theme of her understanding her racial composition as being split or in halves. In her mind, this moment was a fissure in the whole of her identity. As previously mentioned, Jayden had naturally adopted her mother's ethnic and racial identity as her own. She was aware of the racial difference between them but at Jayden's young age the distinction did not fully resonate. "That was the first moment where my African-American side [came out] and [I] felt there was some kind of conflict" (Jayden). The reading of Martin Luther King exposed Jayden to (or clarified for her) the difficult reality of racial tension and violence that is inextricable from US history. Being aware that she was adopted and African American, Jayden clearly had complex reactions to this racial history.

I argue this troublesomeness is comprised of emotional complexity and conceptual absurdity.

> I had known my dad was black. But I never really thought much of it. Like, I knew I got my hair from him and my skin tone was a mixture. But, like, nothing else really hit me on that. But then, when I realized that I know black people who were getting dissed or something, suddenly, it was, like, my problem now. (Jayden)

In other words, Jayden's awareness of her racial composition was heightened in the context of historical tension. Jayden clearly loves and values her mother, but this moment put her in touch with two racial identities which by her description was a moment "where all the confusion started" (Jayden). Jayden even briefly blames her mother (as a representative of white people) for the racial difficulty she learned about. I am not sure as to the degree her age had impact upon the moment of troublesomeness, but the affective element and the conceptual absurdity clearly caused Jayden to see black and white as distinct racial identities.

Jayden discusses how she switched from private to public schools (for middle school) and the difference between the two environments was very striking to her. Jayden states that during this time she changed from "wanting to be all white to wanting to completely belong to a black friend group." Jayden is explicit about not knowing why she experienced these feelings, but she soon belonged to a black friend group exclusively. Moreover, Jayden states: "In order to make sure that I was accepted, I didn't want to be, like, just that one friend that wasn't black. I had to be black just like them. I changed what I did with my hair. I tried cornrows a very brief time. I hated it. It was horrible. Being tan, like as dark as possible, that was it." Jayden also generated a sketchbook entry that further clarifies just how deeply her acceptance, in appearance, as a black female meant to her.

Transcribed text: In elementary school I was dark. I associated myself with the black group at school. In the shower one day I saw the real color of my skin right between my toes, where the sun doesn't touch. There was instant denial toward the pink flesh color. So, I hid them, keeping myself as dark as possible.

FIGURE 4.1   A page from Jayden sketchbook discussing her differences in skin tone

During the interview, Jayden further elaborates on the experience of seeing the skin color between her toes:

> That's, like, always your natural skin color. Because it's never seen in the sunlight. It was so much lighter than the rest of me. I panicked. I was like, no. This can't be. Like, I must be all dark. But that was a part of my body I was extremely self-conscious about. Because I had to be dark. I had to fit in.

It is clear at this point in Jayden's development she went to great lengths to identify as a black female and the effort focused upon her physical attributes. It is important to acknowledge there is a possible relationship between puberty and other normal aspects of individuals changing into teenagers that overlap or explain some of these feelings of insecurity and awkwardness. More specifically, Jayden was exhibiting an insecurity about her physical appearance regarding being accepted by the peers that were important to her. It is reasonable to explain this insecurity as a normal element of adolescent development. However, the shower experience where she obsessed over the pale tone of the skin color between her toes arguably went far beyond feelings of insecurity over friendships and appearance. This experience, as Jayden suggests, is indicative of a deep need for her entirety to be accepted as black, to be identified by her black peers at school as black: "I didn't want to be the single white friend in a black friend group, I wanted be black and accepted as black" (Jayden). In contrast, Jayden acted and spoke in the way she had always done with her mother at home. This was in a sense a duality of identity and persona. It can be argued that at this point in her life Jayden was not necessarily denying her white identity; rather, Jayden was vacillating between her racial identities. More specifically, Jayden felt a need to embrace and develop her black identity; as previously stated, Jayden consistently refers to having a "white side and a black side."

Jayden discussed her language as part of an effort to be black. Therefore, in addition to the changes in her appearance she also spoke in Ebonics. Ogbu (1999) describes Ebonics as a dialect of English that was spoken by black people in the United States. Jayden claims she only spoke like that (Ebonics) at school and at home she spoke in a standard American speech pattern. This is further evidence of a dichotomy of identity as well as a sense of self. The embracing of a language is a means of expressing one's sense of experience, feelings, and state of being. Ebonics is different than slang, which still holds some association with typical white language. As Ogbu (1999) states, Ebonics is a dialect evolved by black America and spoken exclusively by that population as an attempt to separate from the white majority. Jayden's use of this dialect suggests a genuine identification with black identity and a sense of herself as black. In contrast, she spoke in typical dialect or speech patterns when at home with her mother. This, in turn, suggests her identification with her socialized white upbringing.

It is important to note that Jayden did not feel judged or a need to hide anything about her changes in appearance or speech regarding her mother. She always felt her mother accepted her need to explore different aspects of her personality regarding styles, appearance, and even speech patterns. However, at home her speech and behavior were more typical of her upbringing and different from what she presented to her friend group.

In both the interviews and her sketchbook, Jayden discusses a memory that was particularly painful and troubling that strikes to the heart of her vulnerability and insecurities regarding racial identity. Although Jayden does not remember the exact details, she does recall the basic context of the event:

> I'm not really sure. Maybe I called my mom or something and I did not talk like that [using Ebonics] to my mom. It was mostly at school, because I knew she didn't care what I was. But so, I guess I was talking to her or something and I was speaking, like, whatever, and one of the girls in the group called me an Oreo. And, that's when, like, it's such a silly name, but at the time it was so hurtful, like, implying I was only black on the outside and white on the inside. And, that seemed, like, such an insult, because, I guess, even though I put on this whole guise as a black person, I think I became very proud of what I was. Even though, I guess, there's a lot of negative stereotypes about it, I still became very proud to be a black person. And so, when someone told me that I wasn't [black], that I was just a fake, it really hurt.

Jayden continues her reflection upon this event by explaining how she shook the comment off, in the moment. However, it struck her more deeply: "I knew I was like, yeah, that's me, that's pretty much what I am." Jayden goes on to describe feelings of being exposed as her efforts to become "black" was her personal secret. "I guess I just thought it was a bad thing in my head, to be so dark looking on the outside, but so white on the inside."

Erikson (1963) provides insight into how adolescents form independent identities that are autonomous from others and establish bonds with those of the same and other genders. Sue (1981, cited in Poston, 1990, p. 152) states: "Racial identity development is defined as developing pride in one's racial and cultural identity." Poston (1990) states that racial identity formation is important because it develops attitudes about the self, as well as attitudes toward others in the same racial group and the majority. Poston (1990, p. 152) further argues that racial identity formation also "dispels the cultural conformity myth, that is, that all individuals of a particular minority group are the same." This literature partly explains the hurt that Jayden felt in response to the Oreo comment because racial identity forms attitudes about the self. More importantly Jayden is explicit in the importance of being accepted by her black peers as being black. The Oreo comment is clearly a rejection from the black peer group from which she desires acceptance. The comment is particularly hurtful because it touches the core of Jayden's upbringing and her insecurities associated with wanting to be accepted as black. As a result, this compounds Jayden's feelings of being two halves which prevented or complicated some aspects of this identification process.

It is clear that Jayden had developed a sense of pride in her racial identity as both white and black. However, Jayden has encountered many hurtful statements from individuals in her social circles. It can be argued that these hurtful comments had a clear impact upon her understanding of self, regarding the affective dimension. More specifically, her feelings of being exposed (as mentioned previously) resulted in feelings of insecurity and self-doubt continuing for many years. Jayden's sketchbook provides a little more insight regarding some of these experiences regarding her adoptive family.

Transcribed text: 6th grade – My grandpa was not tolerant of any race but his own. At the dinner table he'd often go on little rants but one day he was very blunt and asked me if the people I knew had big lips. This was one of many accounts with my family's lack of tolerance.

FIGURE 4.2   A page from Jayden's sketchbook about a memory of her grandfather making racist remarks about her

Transcribed text: Oreo – an insulting term often used by blacks to derogate other blacks as "black on the outside, white on the inside." White on the inside meaning anything from speaking proper English, getting good grades, liking music other than rap/hip hop and having diverse friend groups. When walking through our halls I am never stopped and told to have a nice day. MY EXPERIENCES. Because my speech is not "ghetto" and I do not dress [in] stereotypical "black women" clothing, my peers assume I hold no ethnic traits. They are surprised when they see my music. When I get a mediocre or bad grade, they claim "but you're mostly white." My only black assets are apparently my butt and my curly hair otherwise people view me as a tan white girl. My boyfriend even states I'm glad you're only half black when we pass a loud group of girls. Many assume I can or cannot dance based on what race they identify me with. The one area I get "looks" and compliments all predominantly black is the Bahamas.

FIGURE 4.3   A page from Jayden's sketchbook about a memory of being called an "oreo"

Transcribed text: Being ashamed of my own race. Black side known for being loud, poor, rude, uneducated, unfaithful. White side known for being rich, hierarchy, intolerant, cannot dance/sing, "Marry white to dilute the brown." "You're not like other black people." "Yes, I am mixed." You are whitest black guy I know." The race card.

FIGURE 4.4   A page from Jayden's sketchbook that lists racial stereotypes and comments she encountered

The sketchbook pages (Figure 4.1–4.4) describe encounters with racism which manifest as mean comments or comments underpinned by racial insensitivity. Furthermore, Jayden (through these comments) is subject to racial assumptions by others regarding her character, quality, and taste, despite her daily behavior. In the interview, Jayden spends time discussing her shock at "comments thrown out so easily," although she feels she has become immune to them for the most part. However, Jayden does "sit back and realize what people will actually say to each other and not think that it's offensive" (Jayden). She states that this form of expressed racism is pervasive and multidirectional, meaning that it is not just white people passing comments about black people. She states that black people are racist toward black people as well as the normal understanding of racism (white toward black). Her point is that the more open discourse had an impact on her by not only magnifying her feelings of being split, but by making her feel that that one side of her (one racial background) was better than the other. As discussed below, some of the comments she encounters reinforce the experience of a split self, such as that her white side was solely responsible for her academic success and ambition.

More specifically, she stated:

> For some reason, I think a lot of mixed kids have this issue, where sometimes, I've met some people who are like that, but for a good portion [of the time], you feel that one race is better than the other. And, I can't really explain why. I think it might be that, maybe the area where you're brought up. Because, obviously, environment has an influence on a lot of things.

Jayden goes on to describe issues of "privilege" being afforded regarding better treatment on job interviews, but on the dance floor she "wants her black side to kick in." Jayden describes this as a conflict in "this side has something better, but then this side has something better, too." "So sometimes there are moments where you forget to mix them and say, like, oh, this is awesome. And you kind of separate them both and say one's better than the other."

Although Jayden has had racist and hurtful encounters, she clearly has also acknowledged positive attributes associated with different aspects of her racial traits. In fact, in her description she actively wishes to exploit them at opportune moments. However, Jayden also describes the embracing of attributes as engaging her white side or her black side kicking in. For example, she discusses her ability to dance or physical attributes (curvy figure and curly hair) associated with black features are aspects she finds positive and flattering. Conversely, her success in school and highly articulate speech are indicative of an educated and sophisticated young woman upon which she places value. Jayden is still not a nuanced individual who is rich in heritage and experience, but a white and black version of herself who finds it beneficial to embrace different racial associations in order to successfully navigate different social contexts. The implication highlights the reality that Jayden seems to lack a holistic self and holds compartmentalized versions of a self that might be connected or situational.

3   Jayden's Artwork and the Liminal Space

Jayden articulates the experience of feelings of racial halves which implies understanding that is represented in her artwork. During her experiences throughout childhood and high school Jayden did not possess the language to express the depth of feeling and conflict she was experiencing. The affective component arguably has an impact on the cognitive understanding to form linguistic signs or signifiers. More importantly, the art-making process provided a means for knowledge construction that involved both the affective and cognitive dimensions.

The relevance of semiotic theory to this case study and this book is the inherent ability to form signs and signifiers that benefit knowledge construction and that is inhibited by aspects of troublesomeness. More specifically, Jayden discusses a friendship with a mixed-race male whom she met during her high school years. She describes an important role of her friendship with the young man as being a venting session based on jokes they both know aren't completely funny. In other words, there is truth to the issues they both face, but the humor makes light of the more serious aspect. The significance of this point is Jayden makes a distinction between venting with this young man about her racial issues and engaging with them in her artwork. "Well, I would say a venting session. It's for me personally. It would be more that I could share it with someone who I know had experienced it, too" (Jayden). She goes on to say, "I wasn't trying to solve anything with it. It was just nice to get it out in the open." It can be argued that these venting sessions were another means to address the unpleasant feelings of the liminal state, especially when language to address the complexity of the issues was not formulated. Furthermore, Jayden describes the role of art making in distinction to a venting session:

> With my art, I was trying to find who I was, I guess. I was trying, like, to say, well, am I black or am I white? Like, I really wanted to know, like, where both sides met up. So, I think that's when I started, that's when I started trying to address it, and that's when I, when it all started – when I met my dad. (Jayden)

Obviously, the second experience that profoundly influenced her artwork was the meeting with her birth father. It was during the winter break of her junior year and members of her adoptive and biological family were present. Jayden remembers it as being strange, and she was very insecure as to whether her biological family would accept her, based on her upbringing and skin color. The interview clearly reveals this meeting carried great significance for Jayden, in being accepted for change and not seen as inferior because of her racial composition. She describes the meeting as going very well and it being another moment of profound change in her. Jayden said she felt complete acceptance from her father and biological family members present at the meeting: "Walking away from this moment, I just really wanted to know, like, why was this a problem with me?" (Jayden). More specifically, walking away from this meeting, Jayden wandered why she still had a problem with the racial experiences in her past.

Clearly, meeting her birth father provided feelings of acceptance on a deep level that I argue provided a form of permission for her to move forward. It is essential that Jayden's linguistic insight into these moments is in retrospect. In other words, the understanding that resulted from these experiences (in the moment) occurred through the affective dimension and it was her art making that allowed a processing of these feelings and provided a semiotic navigation of the liminal state. Jayden claims she did not start making art expecting any profound changes in her life, but when she came back to school after meeting her father, she now realizes she immediately began engaging with these feelings she had about her father and herself. Considering the semiotic lens, Jayden's art portfolio demonstrates a dramatic switch in the use of signs, which clearly correlates to this experience of meeting her biological family. The next section in this chapter provides visual evidence of this semiotic journey.

Land, Rattray, and Vivian (2014) focus on semiotic issues in relation to the liminal state. Jayden is engaging with deep complex feelings that directly impact on her understanding of her place in her world. It can be argued that Jayden may not have had the linguistic means of forming or articulating thoughts in this liminal state for many years. This is in part due to a lack of support or trust in others to help her formulate the language toward understanding.

During our second interview, Jayden describes the content of her artwork as having to "do with the personal transformation and the personal journey of trying to identify with myself as a biracial child" (Jayden). Jayden goes on to state: "Each piece has a personal message or a personal story that I have experienced. Mostly in the past; there are some recent things. But each time I do something, it's just kind of, like, a relief. That's the only reason I do my artwork, I think."

Considering this evolved understanding about her work, Jayden discovered purpose within the art-making process. She clearly states the positive way art making engages the affective dimension. Furthermore, Jayden implies the epistemic value of her art-making process in the evolved cognitive engagement with her past experiences and feelings. This is evidenced by her ability to articulate meaning and use linguistic signs. Although tacit, Jayden was able to employ the art-making process as a vehicle to navigate through the liminal state and cross thresholds related to identity and self.

The following section presents the art portfolio that Jayden submitted for external assessment. In Jayden's view it contains with works that best represent the focus and quality of her artwork. The art portfolio provides a visual representation of Jayden's semiotic navigation of liminality.

4 Jayden's Art Portfolio

Jayden's artist statement submitted for external assessment:

> A little over two years ago, I met my birth father, Robert, for the first time. My nerves stemmed from the fact that he is an African American who was raised in Philadelphia and I am a biracial adoptee who was raised in a white household. The overall experience of meeting Robert was amazing

because I can now say that I know where I get my features and mannerisms. The meeting also raised a very serious and unanswered question, am I Black or White?

After my encounter with my father, all I could paint were up close profiles of various African men. I had no explanation for my new fascination until I remembered the stories that my mother made up about a distant tribe in Africa that my birth family belonged to. I realized that I was looking for a connection between myself and my father and once I was able to satisfy that need, I could expand my understanding of my other inner-racial issues. My new mission was to get a better idea of why I could never settle on what my personal identity is (racially).

My research focuses on the thought processes I went to in order to accomplish this task. I had to know what I approved and disapproved of for both of my halves. Once I could accept the faults and benefits of both I was able to open my mind to the types of artworks that I could create. I no longer feel like I must hold back for fear of offending someone or of touching on an area that is still too sore for me. Everything is out, resulting in my growth and acceptance of who I am. I would not have made any of the necessary connections without my art.

These pieces are entitled *Blackface* (Figure 4.5) and *Nigg* (Figure 4.6), which is two sides of a single sheet of poster board. There are clear references to racist practices and thinking, but they are interwoven with Jayden's sense of experience and feeling. More specifically, blackface (in the United States) was a form

FIGURE 4.5
"Blackface" mixed media on poster boards

JAYDEN: A SPLIT SELF   73

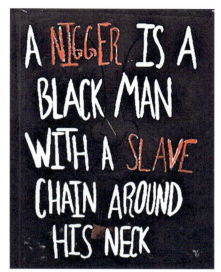 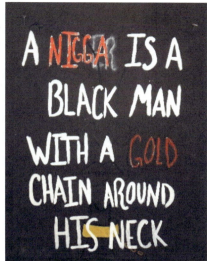

FIGURE 4.6   "Nigg" double sided mixed media artwork on poster board

of theatrical makeup and a form of entertainment in the nineteenth century and into the twentieth century. White actors would wear makeup to give them the appearance of being black. The actors would then act like fools, referencing the black race as lacking intelligence and common sense. Jayden, however, reverses the historical roles and covers the faces so that they have the appearance of being white. When considering her Oreo experience, the piece is clearly expressive of difficult feelings regarding her appearance and racial composition.

Nigga makes use of the most difficult and sensitive of racial slurs. As previously stated, the piece is two sided and the words are a quote from a famous rap artist, Tupac Shakur, which he believes explains the difference between the terms "nigger" and "nigga." In the United States the term "nigga" is often used among black males as a term for friendship, however, many people (including African Americans) find it offensive as well. In this piece, Jayden writes in white the "er" which is the most offensive of the syllables. The piece is highlighting a fine line of offensive language and the associated racial boundary. However, Jayden is also suggesting that although a syllable may have changed the meaning is the same.

These pieces represent a layering of races that lack harmony but rather suggest conflict. In *Blackface*, Jayden is layering her racial components and recontextualizing the humiliation and shame into her own sense of experience and feeling. By using both sides of the board, *Nigg* suggests opposite or even a change in time or context. However, the use of similar elements of design suggests a strong similarity, as if to say nothing has changed. The only distinction is the almost transparent white letters that change the important pronunciation. Jayden seems to be addressing the many absurd and hurtful assumptions made about her throughout her life as they apply to her identity.

These drawings are titled *Inner Warrior* (Figure 4.7), *Jazzy Resentment* (Figure 4.8), and *Killer of* (Figure 4.9) and are fitting of the descriptions of the

FIGURE 4.7   "Inner Warrior" mixed media on paper

FIGURE 4.8   "Jazzy Resentment" mixed media on paper

FIGURE 4.9
"Killer of" mixed media on paper

JAYDEN: A SPLIT SELF

work Jayden says she completed upon the return from meeting her father. They refer to both tribal and urban black males. Jayden states that upon her return she became obsessed with drawing black faces, but she did not make an immediate conscious connection between the drawing process and the "profound life experience" she had just undergone. The tribal figures are indicative of being in a process of construction or destruction. The middle figure is clearly located in a context, but the others are more ambiguous in their state. The middle figure also has a racial reference to a time in the United States in the 1920s and 1930s known as the Harlem Renaissance, which was a period of explosive creative energy in the African-American community located in Harlem; much of the work created at that time had a social conscience. Taking these references into account, it can be argued that these drawings are suggestive of a rethinking or reconfiguration. More specifically, Jayden is undergoing a semiotic processing where the visual representation is a means of understanding or processing the nuance of her father's heritage despite her lack of awareness of her interest in these aspects of him.

Figures 4.10 and 4.11 are entitled *Two Faced* and *Better*, which are clearly like the other drawings of black males but with important distinctions. These two works have clear visual and linguistic references to the face being split or in halves. This references Jayden's own understanding of her racial composition and is indicative of her work becoming expressive of her internal experience as opposed to being about her father or someone else. Furthermore, the drawing on the right, *Better*, makes clear references to mixed race in regard to the different color tones used for skin and the black and gray or lighter eye. Moreover,

FIGURE 4.10   "Two Faced" paint on paper

FIGURE 4.11   "Better" mixed media on paper

FIGURE 4.12 "Purity" hemp glued to paper

FIGURE 4.13 A page from Jayden's sketchbook discussing hair as an important element in racial identity

the darker skin tone is on the side with the lighter eye and the lighter skin tone is on the side with the darker eye. This is suggestive of Jayden's sense of becoming whole or unifying her racial composition within her own understanding. The title of the work is also consistent with these observations. The other drawing in this pair, *Two Faced*, is a distorted and even abstracted black face. The visual element that bisects the drawing has a design reminiscent of tribal design and, arguably, African design. This drawing is suggestive of a changing composition in a literal and personal meaning of the word. The bisecting element seems to create a distortion and is an abrupt or powerful element in the drawing. This can be related to the power of meeting and being accepted by her father. This realization by Jayden is a result of analysis of her current work and making the connection of consistent representation of black male portraits after meeting her birth father.

Purity is the only piece to this point that uses a female subject matter. The piece is made with hemp glued onto paper, which leaves the silhouette of a bald (presumably) African female, although she is the white of the paper. In her sketchbook, Jayden writes about hair as an important element of racial identity and is critical of the common use of hair products by some women to straighten their hair or alter it in some way to make it more acceptable. Jayden references how slaves would attempt to change their hair to appeal to their masters. In conversations with Jayden, she also referred to African tribal women who had shaved their heads and how beautiful she found that. The distinction in the two scenarios in the motivation for manipulating one's hair provides insight into this piece. The figure surrounded by hemp is a reference to more primitive materials and the figure is clearly African and female. It is unusual for Jayden to use female subject matter and the title of this piece (*Purity*) is suggestive of a journey inward. It can be argued that this piece is a more honest conversation regarding what is beautiful regarding her true self.

The final and (by her description) most important piece is *Black Transformation* (Figure 4.14). It is represented here by film stills from a video of Jayden applying paint to her face, neck, and shoulders and then removing it. The video is 2 minutes and 24 seconds in length and is looped in order to play continuously, restarting automatically when the video completes. The artwork is comprised

FIGURE 4.14   "Black Transformation" stills from a 2:24 video of Jayden applying paint to her face, neck and shoulders and then removing it

of still photographs that are put into a video program that sequences through them at the rate of speed Jayden felt was most effective. The video documents Jayden applying paint that references African American skin color and then removing it with a towel. The expression on her face during this process shows strain and relief, which was an issue of primary importance to Jayden.

The applying of paint and its removal is clearly an activity of profound expressive value for Jayden. In her words, the piece is an

> obvious transformation of going from myself to black to back to myself, like a natural physical transformation. And then there was the personal inner-accepting transformation, I guess. [...] I would say from elementary school, from the moment the girl called me an Oreo, there's been an overall transformation of how I feel about myself. And that's what I tried to show through those pictures, because I don't know if other people can tell, like, once, the paint's completely off, like, I'm content, I'm really happy. (Jayden)

Jayden visually represents these obvious and more profound transformations in a powerful and emotional way. The visual metaphor of applying dark paint is a consistent choice in her sense of identifying as white person as a young child and then discovering and engaging with a black identity. Moreover, the facial features and the effort it takes to wipe the paint from her face and neck clearly depict struggle. When one considers the visual representation of identity as well as the depiction of struggle, the piece makes an inner dialogue visual. The psychological and emotional torment experienced by Jayden was most often internal and resulted in questions about identity and self she was not able to verbalize. More importantly, in this artwork Jayden relives her painful moments and documents a personal transformation over time, but the meaning of her experiences reaches new clarity as she is engaging in this expressive act.

In our interviews I asked Jayden if the piece is a literal moment of transformation or if it documents a transformation over a longer period. This is what she said:

> I think it was over a period. It was pointing [to the time] during [which] I really felt it again. Like, kind of like a reminder of everything. But, I just, because it's been such a long process and I knew before that point I'd overcome a lot. So, I just kind of wanted to condense it into a single piece. [...] I just wanted to, like, have an overall thing that could show how I was feeling. (Jayden)

During a discussion about the video piece, Jayden elaborates that the piece was originally just a test to see what the colors would look like on camera and in conversation with me she made important revelations about the work.

> And then you asked if I could put it into a series of, like, like a video, and once I saw it in that, I realized this is awesome, like, this says everything I've been going through. And, just like a series of, like, 200 pictures or something. [...] And then, like, I was thinking about it more, like, if in some faces I could remember what I was thinking, I guess. Like, the one, like the last one where I'm, like, my hair's all messed up and I have everything off and I just have, like, this silly smile, like, in that moment, I remember that I was, like, "This is good," like, "I feel great right now." And it wasn't just because the paint was all gone, yeah, a little bit, but, I mean, it was more of thinking back to, I guess, just like accepting myself, like, I just felt awesome. (Jayden)

Jayden continues to speak in the interview that part of being human is to have flaws or aspects we do not like about ourselves and we need to accept ourselves a little more each day. In reference to the piece and the notion of acceptance, Jayden states:

> I'm sure in another five years, like, I'll probably be making another piece and have, like, another totally aha moment about something. Because, that, I think that one mostly was, not just, like, skin tone. I think, like, a big thing about it was skin tone and just, like, fully accepting myself as a mixed person.

Jayden clearly describes the making of the piece as an intentional visual metaphor for her struggle with racial identity. However, it is also very clear that the making of the artwork and viewing it in a video format allowed her to arrive at a new meaning of the piece and her sense of self. In other words, Jayden used and constructed visual elements to express a state of being but in doing so she crossed through a threshold that allowed for a linguistic description of her struggles with identity and self.

References

Berger, P. L., & Luckmann, T. (1966). *The social construction of reality: A treatise in the sociology of knowledge.* Anchor.

Erikson, E. H. (1963). *Childhood and society.* Norton.

Land, R., Rattray, J., & Vivian, P. (2014). Learning in the liminal space: A semiotic approach to threshold concepts. *Higher Education, 67*(2), 199–217.

Ogbu, J. U. (1999). Beyond language: Ebonics, proper English, and identity in a Black-American speech community. *American Educational Research Journal, 36*(2), 147–184.

Poston, W. C. (1990). The biracial identity development. *Journal of Counseling and Development, 69*, 152–155.

Sue, D. W. (1981). *Counseling the culturally different: Theory and practice.* Wiley.

CHAPTER 5

Aline: "I'm Just Hoping I Can Stop Surviving and Start Living"

1   Introduction

The young woman who is the focus of the case study in this chapter is named Aline. I met her during her senior year, which was her second year back in public school. Prior to this she was institutionalized due to severe psychological issues and self-harm. I was not aware of the full extent of her issues when I first met her and the importance of forming trust in working with Aline. Aline had developed a profound mistrust for adults and institutions, based on her experiences. She discussed the significance of bonding with me regarding her expressing openly.

As I developed a relationship with Aline, we were able to spark an expressive interest and direction for her work. Unfortunately, Aline suffered profound trauma as a young child and her struggles with this trauma became a focus for her work. In fact, I argue it was essential for Aline to engage with these feelings and experiences through the visual art-making process in order to facilitate her healing.

As Aline explains, she experienced several profound moments of betrayal when she was young, which arguably acted as a catalyst for her psychological pain and practice of self-harm. Aline was abused by her father and his friends, however, when she finally talked about the issues with her mother, she was told to never speak of it. As the chapter discusses, this directive to maintain silence impacted Aline the most, according to her accounts. As a result, she maintained silence and her expression of the associated trauma manifested in a destructive manner.

As a result of my bonding with Aline, she began to express her feelings and experiences in an explicit and unapologetic manner. As outlined in Chapter 3, I was ethically obliged to act for Aline and I set up a support system for her. More specifically, I alerted the school psychologists and counselors. Moreover, I contacted her father (with whom she resided) and informed him as to the content of her work. This was more an effort to be proactive if Aline experience emotional turmoil more than concern over any bureaucratic policy.

Aline experienced troublesomeness regarding self and identity, which relates to her experiences of trauma and family dysfunction. Moreover, Aline was instructed and socialized at an early age to not give voice to her feelings and experiences of pain. Therefore, linguistic symbols were not only beyond comprehension, but in her case, they were repressed or perceived as negative. In my experience with Aline she employed the art-making process to engage with her past experiences and traversed the liminal space as a means of healing. Her inability to use linguistic signs was remedied within the semiotic lens with nonlinguistic or visual signs. The case study of Aline represents a young woman who traverses liminality and crosses thresholds that involve an experience of healing and voice achieved within the semiotic domain. As a result, Aline undergoes an ontological shift that result in a new self and identity.

The following artist statement and images were submitted by Aline for external assessment. Other images and writing were submitted as well and will be utilized in other aspects of this chapter. I feel it is necessary to immediately provide insight into the profound sense of feeling that colored Aline's experiences and an underpinning element of her daily living, which is best achieved through her expressive work. The piece that is being used to introduce Aline is entitled *Institution*. It is about her experiences in the mental health facility throughout her youth.

> *Institution*
> I constructed this cell out of a 4' × 8' luan sheet and painted it white to mimic the environment of the hospital I was institutionalized in, and wrote on the inner walls to represent the feelings that arose during my stay first. I used black marker and pencil to create mostly uniform, neat phrases. At some point, I started changing my strokes, using darker and heavier marks, making them more distressed. Initially I was confident I would be able to resurface the emotions needed to produce the results I intended in the piece, but once inside my structure it was very difficult

FIGURE 5.1 "Institution" view of the finished installation

FIGURE 5.2 "Institution" detail shot of the markings on the inside to pull forth things I had kept hidden for so long. It wasn't until I sat in the corner, closed my eyes and tried to remember trauma from my past that I finally opened. I moved to using a paintbrush, then finger-painting and clawing on the walls, which felt more like a true release of the pain and anxiety I experienced. After completing the piece, I realized the build of intensity as the project progressed matched the downward spiral of my mental condition the longer I was forced to stay in the hospital.

Apart from the reference to her time in the mental institutions, the statement hints at her liminal journey and the use of visual and linguistic signs to reengage the affective dimension associated with past experiences. I argue that the re-creation of the cell is more than a memory, but is a semiotic representation of the psychological and emotional silence imposed on her by her mother. In other words, Aline represented the cage she had been in since the time of her abuse and when she told her mother about it. Later in this chapter there will be a description and discussion of the process that is integral to the creation of this piece that far exceeds the labor of construction. The process is one of a liminal navigation that is achieved in a powerful experience of several days.

2 Aline's History, Artwork, and Finding of Voice

The previous section established an introduction of Aline that went beyond the details of her traumatic past and represents her ontological state. The purpose of this approach is to show the images of the installation, which provide a deeper view into her internal experience and some insight as to the psychological and emotional turmoil Aline carries with her. In this section, I will provide a more detailed description of Aline's past experiences along with some of her artwork and writing. The intention of this section is to represent the facilitation of Aline's expressive voice through linguistic and visual signs. The previous section introduces the significance and lasting impact of the imposed silence and abuse on Aline, which I describe as a lack of voice. As Aline began to trust me and engage in art making, she created powerful visual representations that facilitated her engagement with the affective elements of her liminal state.

"I first started self-harming around like, sixth grade. But I remember, like, I started cutting in eighth grade. And it was just, I became, like, obsessed with hurting myself" (Aline). Aline characterizes herself as not having family or friends and she describes her act of cutting as "part of me – it was the only thing that kept me on this earth" (Aline). When one considers this statement more deeply, Aline has developed a cyclical relationship with self-harm. It can be argued that due to a lack of words there is a reliance on a familiar or satisfying action to address the feelings integral to the liminal state (Land, 2014). More specifically, the cyclical relationship with cutting refers to what Land (2014) states in terms of individuals relying on ineffective behaviors to relieve the discomfort of the liminal state. In other words, the lasting affective impact of Aline's past trauma has kept her in a liminal state for many years and the act of cutting was her only approach to relieving the pain and torment she continually experiences. According to Land (2014), individuals can continually employ behaviors or actions (in Aline's case, cutting) despite the fact they are ineffective.

In ninth grade Aline was hospitalized due to accidentally cutting too deep and hitting a vein and was admitted to the psychiatric ward. She states that she was hospitalized three more times in the same year and the hospitalizations continued the following year for suicidal thoughts and depression. Aline describes being heavily medicated "to the point where, like, I didn't, if I wasn't sad, I just didn't have emotions. I was completely numb. It made me feel like a robot." Aline would frequently express an extreme distaste and lack of trust with the mental health institution and associated professionals. In her mind the professionals were a form of drug pusher and did not possess a genuine concern for her or her well-being. The following excerpts are from Aline's sketchbook and they provide insight into her experiences and feelings regarding her hospitalization.

Transcribed text: Doctors didn't want me to contaminate the other patients. I had a room with a bed and a shower. I wasn't allowed any visitors. 3 times a day a nurse would dress up in a plastic suit and slide a tray under my door of food (usually cold or three slices of bread). I wasn't allowed to lay in bed because they didn't want me to develop another illness, so they made me sit in a chair and think about my depression. One day I hid a plastic spoon from my lunch and used it to scratch the skin off my wrist. After that they watched me eat to make sure I didn't "try anything" again. By my second trip to the mental hospital. I was on 7 different kinds of prescription medications. The naltrexone made me tired and my stomach hurt. The ability kept me awake and jittery. The Ativan made me dizzy and unaware of my surroundings (I only took it when I was having anxiety/panic attacks). The Wellbutrin made me a little Hungary and veryjittery. The trazadone made me sleep a little, but it made me sleepy the rest of the time. The Seroquel made me pass out. I wouldn't be able to wake up or think clearly. While slightly numbing my depression these medications also numbed my thoughts, I couldn't converse [or] ate with people because I couldn't really come up with original thoughts and if I did, I couldn't really express them. The worst medicine was Prozac. When I first took it, I got hot flashes, mood swings and nausea, decreased appetite and panic attacks. After my body became more immune to the Prozac and my dose increased, I started to feel like a robot. I did what I was told with no resistance. I didn't feel like a person but a physical body to maintain. What happens when you leave a sad person alone with their thoughts?

FIGURE 5.3   A page from Aline's sketchbook recalling some difficult experiences in a mental health hospital

ALINE: "I'M JUST HOPING I CAN STOP SURVIVING AND START LIVING"   85

Transcribed text: Take all my things and throw them around the room. Sometimes she broke vases against walls or held a knife to her wrist laughing hysterically screaming I'll do it. But they all expected and wanted me to live a normal life free from pain, sadness or concern. I didn't know who or what I was [and] that every moment I was alive I was in unbearable pain. The only way to escape it was to cut myself or think about suicide. I wasn't a functioning person and I didn't see a need to live.

FIGURE 5.4   A page from Alines sketchbook reflecting on her suicidal thoughts and cutting

Transcribed text: People say they care or that they'll listen but so many times I tried to tell someone. They hear noise come out of your mouth, but they don't listen to what words you say. They sit and tell you how to feel better and it makes them feel better, but you never do, and it gets so lonely. After they talk at you for so long, they get frustrated because you don't feel better, so they leave. No one wants to be around a sad person: Dominion never helped me. I was committed so I could work through my depression with professional help but all they did was give me pills and lock me in my room. I sat alone in my thoughts for so long. There was nothing else to do. I sat and thought about my parents, my life and myself. I drove myself near insanity. "If you're not crazy when you come in you will be when you get out" (on several walls written or scratched in the hospital). Although we lived among other people in the ward, we were encouraged not to make any connection or bond with other patients.

FIGURE 5.5   A page from Aline's sketchbook reflecting upon her lack of faith in the mental health system

These excerpts from Aline's sketchbook suggest a hopeless and even cynical perception of the hospital as a place of incarceration rather than a place of healing. It can be argued that due to the profound impact upon the affective dimension that Aline was simply incapable of entering or even comprehending a construct of healing. Moreover, in her mind it was a battle of an institution trying to forcibly make her "live a normal life free from pain, concern or sadness" and her natural impulse to self-harm or indulge suicidal thoughts, which was her only coping mechanism for addressing her turmoil.

Figure 5.6 is a graphite drawing Aline submitted as part of her art portfolio and was part of her sketchbook. The image of self-harm and cutting is the obvious topic but there are several contrasts that suggest the image is not just an illustration of self-harm but of the medicated state she discusses in her writings and the experience of the hospital itself. More specifically, she presents herself in the hospital clothes she describes and there is a sense of sterility to the implied environment. More importantly, there is a stark contrast between

FIGURE 5.6
A graphite drawing executed in Aline's sketchbook and submitted as part of her portfolio

the extremely violent plunging of the knife into her wrist and the somewhat expressionless face that is being manipulated by puppet strings. The pulling of the puppet strings forces a smile upon the figure's face as the corners of her mouth and her eyes are being forcibly held open. This is consistent with her description of the medicated state where she is "robotic" and incapable of feeling unless it is pain or sadness. The female in the drawing has an almost vacant but crazed stare with signs of humanity as indicated by the tear and arguably the act of cutting itself. In other words, Aline is representing the "robotic" state she explicitly attributes to the medications she was taking, but it also suggests the act of self-harm is also "robotic." More specifically, the drawing suggests the knife is plunged deep into the wrist without hesitation or fear on the part of the young woman in the drawing. When considering Aline's description of herself, her only sense of feeling was sadness and pain. When not medicated, the act of cutting is her natural or automatic response.

Implicit in Aline's experience with the hospitals is an obvious sense of hopelessness, but, more importantly, a lack of voice. She consistently references the isolation and lack of communication in a literal sense. Another form of isolation and feeling voiceless is not being heard or understood in therapy sessions, more specifically, being talked at or told how to behave. Aline interpreted these as disingenuous concern or selfish attempts for others to feel better about her. Furthermore, the drugs, by her own admission, dulled some of the depressive feelings but her issues were not addressed; they were only treated as a symptom. The drug treatments also further isolated Aline due to her lack of clear thoughts as a result of being in compromised states.

In Aline's junior year, her parents divorced. She describes this as one of the best things that happened in her life. As a result, her mother moved away, and

Aline felt her life had started improving at that point. "It's just once my mother left, like, it felt like this huge blanket had been lifted" (Aline). Aline further explains that she had to drop her mother off in Alabama, which is where her mother lives to this day. Aline chose to live apart from her mother and resides with her father, despite the history of abuse. When Aline returned home, she remembers stepping into her bedroom and "it was just, like, there was something different, I'm not sure. But it just seems like everything was so much better" (Aline). I asked Aline if she had been hospitalized since that day and she responded that she has not. It is important to highlight that Aline at this point in her life is voluntarily living with her father, who was "inappropriate with her at times" (Aline). Yet the absence of her mother is a huge relief and improvement to her life. According to Aline, her mother imposed the emotional weight upon her, which she describes as carrying the emotional weight of two people. Once Aline returned from Alabama, she "didn't have to carry her burdens. I didn't have to care for her" (Aline).

Both of Aline's parents committed a profound betrayal from the perspective of Aline, regarding the abuse as well as the imposed silence. According to Cook et al. (2005, p. 392),

> early caregiving relationships provide the relational context in which children develop the earliest psychological representations of self, other, and self in relation to others. These working models form the foundation of a child's developmental competencies, including tolerance to distress, curiosity, sense of agency, and communication. When the child-caregiver relationship is the source of trauma, the attachment relationship is severely compromised.

Implicit in Cook et al. (2005), there is theoretical evidence of how the traumatic experiences began to impact Aline's sense of self and her ability to connect and form relationships with others. Consequently, she lacked the ability to express and communicate about her troublesome feelings and impulses for self-harm.

When I turned off the camera for this interview session, Aline stated that the school psychologist expressed a deep concern over the lack of adult and parental connections in her life. Aline stated that she is realizing how upset she is over not having parents. "It makes me very sad to not have parents. I don't love my mother. I don't love my father. I don't think I'm capable of loving myself. I don't know what love is, really" (Aline). I responded by saying, "Well, you made a big start by connecting to several adults, myself, the other art teacher and your therapist." Aline smiles and says she is happy. She concluded

FIGURE 5.7   Film stills from a video that depicts a peace symbol made of being incinerated

by saying with a soulful look, "I'm just hoping I can stop surviving and start living. There's a big difference you know" (Aline).

These images are film stills from a video that Aline produced for her portfolio and prior to her main installation work, introduced formerly. I believe the video effectively represents the impact of her childhood experiences in both trite and more subtle ways. The video consists of a wreath of flowers, made by Aline, in the shape of a peace symbol. The figure in the video is Aline's father. He squirts lighter fluid on to the wreath and then ignites it with a match. The video lasts the length of time it takes for the wreath to completely burn to ash. It is significant that Aline used her father in the video and made the film at her house since both are closely involved in her past abuse. The burning of the wreath made of flowers and in the shape of a peace sign is a clear visual representation of Aline's destroyed innocence. Moreover, it is the father that squirts the fuel and ignites the flames that begins the destruction and her innocence being lost – not just in the sexual context, but in the deep betrayal experienced by Aline and the consequence (in her own words) of her not being able to love.

It is worth considering the visual element of letting the flames burn out and extinguish on their own. The logical visual interpretation of the flames burning out is a form of destruction and loss that can never be recovered. In addition, the flames burn for a period while emphasizing the shape of the peace symbol, which suggests a lasting turmoil and pain. I argue the burning is a representation of the traumatic events of Aline's past continuing to burn in her psyche and the affective aspects of self. However, the flames do burn out and there is nothing left. In one sense, this can be understood as the emptiness that Aline feels toward herself and her family. Another interpretation of the flames being burnt out is a lessening of the power of the past events over Aline. More specifically, as Aline engages with these experiences, she is extinguishing the power they have over her. Aline's art-making process and writing about her experiences has provided a voice and a means for her to engage the power of the affective dimension. The artwork that Aline has made thus far is, in my experience, extremely brave and bold, and the use of her father in the video was significant. She could easily have chosen a model that has fewer complex associations to the events about which she was expressing (i.e., a male friend instead of her father). However, the use of her father in the video enhances the expressive power of the work and is indicative of commitment to an expressive representation, which indicates the presence of her voice in the work. In other words, the making of the film had clear affective elements that are inextricable from the worst moments in her life. But Aline chose to use visual elements that represented the truth of her experience as effectively as she could, no matter what discomfort was involved in the making of the artwork. These decisions were clearly hers to make and are suggestive of a young woman who is finding a means to offer voice through semiotic visual signs. As her portfolio evolves, Aline continually engages the art-making process as a means of giving voice to her experiences and act as a semiotic navigation of liminality associated with aspects of self and healing.

3   Aline and the Liminal State

This chapter has established an important relationship between the affective elements of Aline's experiences and aspects of voice to engage and make meaning out of these experiences. I argue that Aline was (and may remain) in a liminal state due to an inability to give voice to profound affective elements associated with her trauma. Meyer and Land (2005) establishes the essential point that threshold crossing would remain a conceptual issue of cognitive organization or perspective if it were not for the element of troublesome knowledge. As argued by Rattray (2016), the crossing of thresholds and the liminal state clearly holds complex emotional components as does the associated transformation to individuals. Aline is struggling with more than acknowledging the reality of her past abuse; she is seeking a means to engage with the emotional components and process them for the sake of healing, which in her case is a profound ontological shift.

Meyer and Land (2006) clarify that individual learners experience differing levels of troublesomeness with different threshold concepts and, by extension, their willingness to engage with them will also fluctuate. Rattray (2016) considers different psychological constructs of hope, optimism, emotional security, and resilience, particularly as they pertain to psychological capital (Luthans and Youssef, 2004; Luthans et al., 2007) as a means of understanding these individual differences to engage with differing levels of troublesomeness.

The case of Aline clearly demonstrates that the construct of troublesome knowledge involves the affective dimension. According to Aline, her willingness to survive and her coping mechanism of self-harm was her sole source of agency.

The issue being highlighted is again found within the art therapy literature. More specifically, Harnden, Rosales, and Greenfield (2004) argue that art making is a means in which depressed persons can release aggression without having to engage in oral communication. Furthermore, Waller (2006, p. 281) states

> that art made in the safe confines of the art therapy room may enable a child to explore and express feelings that cannot easily be put into words. Instead of acting out "difficult" feelings the child puts these into the object. This can then be shared with the therapist. The art can act as a "container" for powerful emotions, and can be a means of communication between child and art therapist.

I argue that the art-making process functioned in a similar way for Aline in that she was able to give voice to complex affective elements using visual signs. This is particularly relevant for Aline as a result of her inability to use linguistic signs due in part to the power of the associated feelings and the negative impact of her mother's command to never speak about her trauma. In short, Aline lacked a vehicle or means for moving beyond her "robotic" behaviors of cutting and self-harm, which Land (2014) describes as a dependence upon familiar courses of action despite evidence of their futility.

The argument being made here is about the role of visual art making as a semiotic navigation of the liminal space. This chapter has established that Aline had an inability to form linguistic signs to engage with her troublesome experiences and, as a result, Aline relied upon cutting as a means of engaging with her feelings. A relevant example is from a conversation earlier in the year, during which Aline had started to cry. When I asked if we needed to stop, she said no, it was a good thing.

> When I was younger, I got into trouble for, like, expressing feelings kind of, or, like, expressing concern with my situation, so I just didn't. And then, I guess, when you're sad all the time, crying just like it doesn't matter. And, I know when I was cutting, it was like a replacement. I know biologically, when we cry, we release, well, it's, like, to release emotions. But, I kind of replaced that with cutting myself and I just felt numb. I didn't, I just couldn't cry. It wasn't, like, that I wasn't sad; it was, like, my sadness was so deep that I just couldn't bring forth tears. And then going back over emotional things earlier with the other interview, I started, or I started crying and it felt good, because there's a lot of things, you know, bottled inside. And then it was released without cutting myself. That was really powerful. (Aline)

Aline is clearly describing a liminal state that is drenched with an affective element and becomes overwhelming. Her description of being scorned for "expressing feeling or concern" arguably magnifies the overwhelming power of these feelings as her ability to engage with them had been impeded. In other words, the liminal tunnel (Rattray, 2016; Vivian, 2012) is arguably deeper and darker for some and the tools employed for its navigation may reside only within oneself, despite the myriad of resources presented. This highlights issues of boundary crossing and the discursive nature of threshold crossing. As Aline began to engage in the art-making process, she was able to give voice to her experiences and their powerful affective elements. I argue that the ability to give voice through her visual signs empowered her art making to act as a semiotic vehicle and navigate her liminal experience. The previous example of Aline forming tears is significant evidence of her beginning to process and make meaning from her experiences, which suggests an ability for ontological shifts or transformation. The next section will address this aspect of her art-making process and threshold crossing.

4   Institution and Healing

As discussed in the former section, a holistic introduction of Aline was best served using some of her artwork. More specifically, the graphite drawing and the video stills were submitted to IB as part of Aline's art portfolio and indicate her giving voice to her experiences and liminal experience. However, the piece presented in the opening paragraphs and accompanied by the artist statement was the focus of Aline's expressive work for most of her year.

There are primary reasons for the length of time involved with this installation. The first was the conceptual component of the piece, which was to relive or arguably reexperience her feelings while in an isolation cell in the mental hospital. This conceptual component involved aspects of design and construction of an isolation cell but also the more complex aspects of conveying and representing these experiences in a compelling manner. Aline and I arrived at the decision of involving the performative element to the piece, which required a great deal of conceptual structure but could be improvised in the creative moment. In other words, time was spent considering the intention of the piece as well as how the performative element would be executed and presented as an artwork. More specifically, the performative element of the artwork was the action of Aline enclosing herself inside the room and engaging in the writing and marking process. As the teacher (with a lot of experience creating performance pieces for my own expressive work), I expose the students to the emotional and conceptual depths of performance art. One rationale for this is performance art often devolves into a form of bad theater and can be glorified as provocative or expressive when the work lack substance. The point being performance art involves an extreme commitment to an expressive activity that the artist finds meaningful and expressive of respective concepts. This commitment to an expressive activity often challenges conventional thought (of the viewer) and can place absurd physical, emotional, or psychological challenges upon the artist performing the work.

Therefore, the primary questions students need to consider when engaging with performance art are: Should I do something in front of an audience? Should I present visual documentation of myself doing something (photo, video, etc.)? Should I leave the evidence of something I did? Obviously, Aline arrived at the latter. Once this primary determination is internalized, the rest of the presentation of the piece becomes a matter of understanding the attitude and implicit logic for it. The affective dimension is part of all performance work as the artist must be prepared to commit without hesitation to the conceptual and visual structure put in place. Obviously, the performance element of the piece directly involves the affective dimension regarding Aline's use of visual art to engage with her experiences.

Institution is the final piece and the primary focus of Aline during her year in IB art.

> I wanted to mimic my experience in a mental institution. [...] The original plan was to construct the sort of cells that I'd be enclosed in. Some[thing] that make the feeling of being trapped inside the hospital. [...] After painting it white, and constructing, putting the cell together, I enclosed myself inside and proceeded to write on the walls thoughts I had while I was in the hospital. Things the doctors, nurses, my parents, other students, and kids I knew had said to me. Everything I had felt, I just kind of tried to express on the wall.

In Aline's case the commitment to her performance involved a great deal of courage and vulnerability. It also required an adherence to ethical principles on my part (as an educator). Obviously, the piece involves much more than writing and sketching things she remembers on the wall. In the context of art criticism, the artwork would be considered a failure if the viewers' experience of the piece remained limited to reading written memories on the wall. The piece transcended this state and involved the reopening of a wound and a reliving of feelings and experiences that are profoundly painful. In my view, I had an ethical obligation to ensure the physical and emotional safety of Aline in the process of her performance. This ethical concern intertwined with some of the practical structures used in executing the piece, as well. After the construction and painting of the structure, Aline and I sat in the exhibition space each evening after school for four days, from approximately 6 pm to 8 pm each night. During this time period Aline would enclose herself inside the structure while I sat in proximity. I would do verbal checks at random intervals to ensure her well-being. At the end of the sessions I waited with Aline until she was picked up to be driven home and would gauge her state of mind as best as possible. It is important to note the discussion on ethics with other steps taken, in the course of the study, such as parent awareness of the artwork being made, in order to meet ethical obligations regarding the student's safety. Aline working in multiple sessions was also a necessary structure as she attempted to consciously enter or acknowledge the liminal tunnel by intentionally engaging with her most painful experiences, giving them visual form and literal representation. As the week went on, the writing and mark making changed radically from being controlled and limited to writing to much more expressive and involving scratches, drawings and handprints. As I sat outside the structure, I often saw it shift and heard noises as the intensity of her physical interaction in the space amplified.

FIGURE 5.8
"Institution" view of the completed installation

As Aline said:

> It was very hard to bring up a lot of the things from my past. Being in the institution in general was a very horrible experience. It was painful to

remember. Not to mention all the things that had put me in there in the first place. But it was [...] after kind of pulling out all the painful experiences and forcing myself to go through that again. When I finally finished, it was so relieving to express some of these things that I've never been able to share. (Aline).

I asked Aline if this is literally the first time, she articulated some of these thoughts and feelings. "Uh huh" (Aline).

FIGURE 5.9   Detail views of "Institution"

In the interview, Aline goes on to describe the role of the visual art-making process in her life over the past year. Aline states that making the artwork combined with her mother's participation in a therapy program has allowed her to understand just how deeply her past had impacted her. Aline was not specific as to the nature or type of therapy program her mother had been attending and she did not bring it up again. This makes sense in the context of our interviews, which began to focus more on her art-making process and less on family relationships and therapy.

In my artwork, I've noticed that, like, a couple of my pieces are kind of graphic, I guess, and I feel like that's a lot of repressed anger that I'm feeling, or repressed sadness that I like to pretend is not there. But as I create the artwork, you know, if it's, like, graphic in nature, it's kind of hard to ignore that repressed, those repressed feelings. And, I guess, just taking an image out of your head and then actually creating it, puts things in a different perspective and it makes you look at what you're thinking in a different way. (Aline)

Implicit in this quote is an element of self-dialogue that is semiotic in nature and provokes Aline to reflect upon the meaning of her experiences. The visual signs that represent the affective dimension associated with her past are given voice and become accessible to her in a manner that is safe and perceptible. In other words, the art-making process acts as a vehicle for the navigation of her liminality because the emotions that were previously overpowering are now able to be engaged with through the semiotic discourse. As a result, Aline talks about a new perspective and is even capable of using linguistic signs in describing her experiences and feelings about them.

"It's really hard for me to communicate how I feel" (Aline). She elaborated on this by saying that given the choice of speaking directly to a person or using artwork she would choose to use her artwork.

I mean, with words, you can say anything and people – they can listen, but that doesn't mean they're going to hear you. But with artwork you can show someone, and images are very powerful, like when you look at something, chances are somewhere in your memory, it's going to be there for the rest of your life. And there's so many things you can say with an image that you can't say with words, that you can't describe with words. (Aline)

Aline alludes to her art making as it relates to self-explanation theory in her conscious decision to engage with ideas that allow her understanding to "kind of expand and grow or become more in-depth." "It's usually a conscious decision but on a few pieces, it was kind of I did it and then I stepped back and I realized, like, it had a deeper meaning than I thought" (Aline).

The conversation then turned to changes she sees in herself since the start of this journey and her art-making experience. The major changes Aline acknowledges in herself is that she is more positive and a lot stronger than she has ever been. Although she acknowledges that there is still work to be done in her healing, she has also formed a trusting relationship with three adults; myself, another art teacher, and her therapist. Consequently, she finds value in communication and she is honest with her therapist and knows how to ask for help when she feels she is at a breaking point. As she said, "I feel very capable of surviving." I asked Aline if she has hope. Aline answered that she is hopeful, but feelings are tricky. She explained that the day her mother left she stopped taking her medicine and she believes that feeling negative and positive emotions is a good thing. The implication points to the impact of her mother upon her ability to engage and process emotions. Moreover, Aline is indicating an ontological shift from being subject to her emotions to being capable or willing to experience them.

The childhood repression of expressing feeling and viewpoints had a profound impact upon Aline and her ability to navigate the liminal tunnel. This is evident, in her discussions, and understanding of her emotional states. This is especially evident when Aline is discussing her art-making process and her understanding of her ability to express her current emotional states. Obviously, the sexual trauma is an egregious and immoral act, but she forced repression of feelings profoundly debilitated her ability to move forward. When Aline discusses her past experiences or her mother or father, she is less articulate. While once again I do not attempt to make causal arguments, clearly Aline has undergone many different treatments and experiences that clearly have facilitated her healing in different ways. But she places clear value on the power of making and experiencing image and the inherent power of expressing the self as means of understanding the self more deeply.

There is clear significance attached to her artwork *Institution* and the experience of its public exhibition. Aline was able to achieve an expressive commitment in representing her most horrible experiences with the knowledge that others would interact with the finished piece. As previously stated, Aline was initially nervous about people seeing her work but found it empowering as the evening unfolded and after it was over. The experience of giving voice that was experienced by others in an authentic manner provided a form of healing for Aline. The acceptance of self that had been disrupted by horrific events found some ability to be whole.

In this case study, Aline clearly struggles with the trauma of the past and the instructions from her mother to maintain silence, no matter the pain. As a result, she became self-destructive and engaged in self-harm; her sense of self was intertwined with the pain as well as the institutions and attempts at self-harm or suicide. The trust formed with me and the more enlightened conceptualization of art as nonlinguistic knowledge provided a semiotic means toward the navigation of liminality, transformation, and threshold crossing. Previously, I discussed the work of Reynolds and Lim (2007) and the use of art for women to engage and reconcile the emotional trauma associated with cancer. Reynolds and Lim (2007) also discuss the observation of women finding purpose in their lives. Furthermore, the art therapy literature claims the need for individuals to generate symbols associated with the liminal state and troublesomeness in a reflexive and symbolic way (Sibbet & Thompson, 2008; Turner, 1995). In other words, Aline was able to benefit from the learning environment to generate art informed by a semiotic lens. I argue this semiotic navigation of the liminal space involved making overpowering emotions accessible and facilitating an ontological shift.

References

Cook, A., et al. (2005). Complex trauma in children and adolescents. *Psychiatric Annals*, *35*(5), 390–398.

Harnden, B., Rosales, A. B., & Greenfield, B. (2004). Outpatient art therapy with a suicidal adolescent female. *The Arts in Psychotherapy*, *31*(3), 165–180.

Land, R. (2014, July). *Liminality close-up* [Paper presentation]. HECU7 at Lancaster University.

Luthans, F., & Youssef, C. M. (2004). Human, social, and now positive psychological capital management: Investing in people for competitive advantage. *Organizational Dynamics*, *33*(2), 143–160.

Luthans, F., Youssef, C. M., & Avolio, B. J. (2007). *Psychological capital*. Oxford University Press.

Meyer, J. H. F., & Land, R. (2005). Threshold concepts and troublesome knowledge (2): Epistemological considerations and a conceptual framework for teaching and learning. *Higher Education*, *49*(3), 373–388. https://doi.org/10.1007/s10734-004-6779-5

Meyer, J. H. F., & Land, R. (Eds.). (2006). *Overcoming barriers to student understanding: Threshold concepts and troublesome knowledge*. Routledge.

Rattray, J. (2016). Affective dimensions of liminality. In R. Land, J. H. F. Meyer, & M. T. Flanagan (Eds.), *Threshold concepts in practice* (pp. 67–76). Sense.

Reynolds, F., & Lim, K. H. (2007). Turning to art as a positive way of living with cancer: A qualitative study of personal motives and contextual influences. *Journal of Positive Psychology*, *2*(1), 66–75.

Sibbett, C., & Thompson, W. (2008). Nettlesome knowledge, liminality and the taboo in cancer and art therapy experiences: Implications for learning and teaching. In R. Land, J. H. F. Meyer, & J. Smith (Eds.), *Threshold concepts within the disciplines* (pp. 227–242). Brill.

Turner, V. (1995). *The ritual process: Structure and anti-structure*. Transaction Publishers.

Vivian, P. (2012). *A new symbol based writing system for use in illustrating basic dynamics* [Unpublished PhD thesis]. Coventry University.

Waller, D. (2006). Art therapy for children: How it leads to change. *Clinical Child Psychology and Psychiatry, 11*(2), 271–282.

CHAPTER 6

Rene: A Conversation with My Subconscious

1 Introduction

The individual who is the focus of this case study is named Rene. I had worked with Rene for several years before she made a conscious transition in her artwork. The interviews with Rene revealed that she had come to learn, in various art courses with me, the dialogic and communicative element of visual art. Rene soon understood that this dialogic element is both expressive to others as well as introspective and reflective. This learning provided empowerment for her to begin navigation of the liminal space and engage with troublesome knowledge.

Rene suffered sexual abuse at the hands of her father when she was younger. As a result, she carried the weight of complex emotions that impacted her sense of self and self-worth. More specifically, Rene discusses the internal desire to be accepting of her past experiences and the realization that she was a victim and not responsible for what happened. However, Rene experienced feelings of guilt and shame as a result of the abuse she suffered. Therefore, the threshold that is pertinent to Rene is relevant to identity that consists of an acceptance of self and healing.

This chapter on Rene provides little or no details of the abuse that she suffered, but focuses entirely on its continual and lasting impact upon the cognitive and affective dimensions of accepting the self. Rene also discusses the inability to form linguistic signs primarily due to inextricable feelings of pain and shame with any words attempted to be communicated. At times, this inability to form linguistic signs is less associated with not having the words but literally an inability to speak them due to the aforementioned affective element. Therefore, Rene provides an interesting and powerful example of a young woman who came to understand the unique ability of visual art to communicate complex feelings and thoughts through nonlinguistic or visual signs. Rene has been able to navigate the liminal space and arguably cross thresholds involving identity and understanding of self.

2 Rene's Portfolio

Rene does not describe in much detail the trauma of her past. Instead, she concentrates primarily on how she utilizes the art-making process to overcome her lingering struggles with her experiences. As she said:

© KONINKLIJKE BRILL NV, LEIDEN, 2022 | DOI:10.1163/9789004508132_006

Well, when I was a kid, my parents got divorced, so, occasionally, I was required to visit my dad and he was a very domineering person. I had problems and it was discovered that I was being abused. It was addressed. I went to court, but it continued to happen for several years. And what my art is about is just about my feelings and the struggle with really being ok with what happened and understanding it wasn't my fault. There wasn't anything I could do with it. And just dealing with the aftermath of what happened. (Rene)

Implicit in this statement are issues of liminality and the affective element resulting in a struggle to accept the self due to the weight of complex emotions. The following artist statement, by Rene, submitted for external assessment, provides an explanation for the underpinning ideas of her submitted art portfolio:

From the beginning, I used my artwork to express the feelings I had that were too difficult to express with words. Things that were too hard to speak. These feelings stem from a childhood of abuse. I started with pieces that only hinted at the feelings I kept hidden, but I soon began to explore my emotions more overtly, and it shows in my work. Through my pieces, I share my darkest days with those who view them. I share my feelings of inadequacy, feelings of shame, and the idea of being the victim. But I also share a light through my work. That shining beam of hope that is recovery, being a survivor.

In some of my pieces I share the idea of being proud of myself, even. However, most of it is about more negative feelings. Some of it is simply about mindset. My sculptures reflect that. The hands sculpture shows the idea of reaching out for help, understanding that you are broken and wanting to be fixed. Many people do not get to that second step of fixing the problem. The other sculpture, the door, is about perception and trust. We are never what we first appear to be, but others must take that first step to open us up to the world. Doors don't simply open themselves.

There is often a contrast in my work, a sort of opposing forces. I first showed this idea in my mural, displaying the negative and the positive sides of one as separate entity. Later, I showed this idea in my photography. In one, I show the contrast between male and female. The other two go as a pair; one of shame and one of pride. This two sidedness shows how I am often conflicted with myself.

Rene describes her art as "a conversation with my subconscious." In her mind, the nature of the art-making process changed from being purely for the release

RENE: A CONVERSATION WITH MY SUBCONSCIOUS   101

of feeling to having ideas she wished to communicate and express. Rene embraces the dialogic element of the art-making process in communicating with others but also as a means of engaging with the self.

> But after a while, I realized that my art was actually telling me something about myself. So, I started looking at it a little further. I knew that some things were sort of similar and there was a common undertone behind it. So, what happened is I started to explore that. That's when I found out art is a way that I was expressing myself in ways I didn't feel comfortable expressing before. It's also a way of me trying to point it out to myself even when I don't know it. I know that sounds very weird but it's how it works. (Rene)

This untitled painting (Figure 6.1) by Rene is an important piece in her development through her years in the art program. This painting is Rene's first successful attempt at communicating her inner struggles with an external audience. More specifically, during the interviews, Rene had told me that it was easier to answer questions about her past than it is to find the words to say and she made this piece with the intention of provoking me into asking questions. Rene told me that she was confident I would have sensed something in the work and begin to ask her about it. Rene was correct; I had immediate concern as to the meaning of the piece. As we critiqued and discussed the work, she

FIGURE 6.1
"Untitled" is a life size painting comprised entirely hand prints on paper

revealed the reality of her past trauma. Therefore, this artwork is a conscious form of dialogue intended to initiate a linguistic exchange with myself about her past. Moreover, it is a conscious use of visual art through a semiotic lens.

The visual elements of the painting present a clear composition of a figure standing and (presumably) waving. There are no clear features that fully define or resolve the figure. In other words, the figure is in flux or a process of taking form. It is also worth noting the figure is greeting the viewer, almost as an invitation or introduction, and when taken in the context, it can be argued we are meeting the "real Rene."

Rene explains that she is interested in the implicit personal association of hand and fingerprints with identity.

> The colors – the parts that are colored and white – they make the outline of myself. This is me. And all the different colors represent different emotions, different feelings I have. And everything that is black is something [that] is not part of me, that isn't the individual colors. And it's just pushing in. It outlines it because it just sort of defines me because [it is] about one point when I was literally defined by other people's feelings, other people's identities. The only thing that is overtly supposed to be free is these hands, which are done in small metallic colors, which, you'll see, there's sort of extra white space around them that isn't oppressed by black. Those sort of really define themselves. So, it's sort of showing how even though being depressed and defined by other people's ideas and identities, I was still able to be myself in a way. (Rene)

Rene is explicit in that she attaches the idea of identity to the hands and the handprint. When one further considers the handprints as a visual element of the painting, issues of intimacy and abuse are also quite explicit. The background

FIGURE 6.2   Details of "Untitled"

is made entirely of black handprints that are layered with an extreme density, causing them to appear as a single opaque tone. The background invades the natural outline of the white figure (with fingerprints), which conveys a feeling of either the figure emerging from the background or potentially in danger of being pulled back into its abyss. Furthermore, the color white, which Rene uses to describe the figure, references purity or virginity. The colorful handprints can be interpreted as a molesting entity, in that they do not belong to the body. They are invasive and even menacing in some cases, appearing to be grabbing or smacking the figure. This is compounded when one considers the figure is white with colored handprints on top. The implication is that white is a natural and pure or innocent state of being.

I find this representation particularly interesting in its subconscious visual reference to a tunnel or space. Although Rene has no academic awareness of threshold concepts, I find this representation a powerful depiction of the affective experience of the liminal space. The quality of the figure being in flux is suggestive of a transformative state which holds significance in the context of the intended communicative element of the work. More specifically, it may be indicative of the willingness to communicate her affective reality.

As previously stated, Rene sees the figure/background relationship as a conflict over identity and, more specifically, as a struggle to resist outside forces and to be self-subscribing. In other words, Rene makes an important distinction between herself as the figure and the other elements of the painting (the color handprints and the background). As she said: "The only thing that is overtly supposed to be free is these hands, which are done in small metallic colors, which, you'll see, there's sort of extra white space around them that isn't oppressed by black." Rene continues by describing these hands as being her own hands, which are the only body part represented in form as the rest of the body is represented as a silhouette. This subtle distinction allows one to interpret issues of power and powerlessness within the artwork regarding the handprints and her use of the hand as an expressive element that holds connotations (Langer, 1942). The relevance of this observation is it suggests a means for Rene to articulate the liminal state and a formation of the self or identity.

Figure 6.3 presents a large mural painted in the main hallway of our high school; it is measured as 88" × 72". The mural consists of two female figures facing each other, presumably a form of mirror image of the same individual. There are obvious differences in the females as one is painted in warm, fleshy tones with a happy expression whereas the other figure is painted in cooler blue tones and is seemingly depressed or sad. The more positive figure is gazing upward as part of her laughing gesture and the more depressive figure is gazing downward. The hair for each figure is long but its movement and form

FIGURE 6.3
Mural that is painted in the main hallway of our school which depicts two female figures facing each other

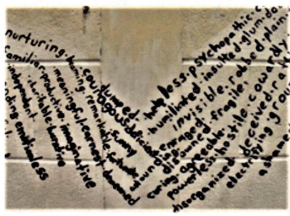

FIGURE 6.4
Detail of the mural that depicts positive and negative attributes overlapping

is not rendered with tones. Instead, the gesture of the hair is filled with words (positive words and negative words in order to match with the respective figure). As the gesture of the hair moves toward the center of the composition the negative and positive words meet but do not blend in a visual way. However, the words do integrate with the opposite side; more specifically, at the bottom some negative words are listed on the positive side and vice versa (Figure 6.4).

> I really tried to show sort of two halves of a person. And how everyone's really sort of put into opposing forces. […] And so, they're, like, looking at each other because you're always working off both halves of yourself. The part that you like and the part that you don't like.

Rene chose this location for the mural because of a natural division that is part of the architecture that creates a visible but not disruptive separation between the figures. "But I could still paint a mural on here as I wanted. So, [I] really showed how it can have one whole. Again, just like everyone has two sides, [a] side they like [and a] side they don't like. But they're still the same person, still interconnected" (Rene).

The use of literal words and the choice to create this work as a public mural holds importance that needs to be considered. As previously discussed, Rene intentionally exploited the dialogic element of visual art as a visual sign to convey powerful feelings she was incapable of expressing in linguistic signs. The previous artwork was created at the end of her junior year; this mural was the primary focus of the beginning of her senior year. There are several murals created by students on the school walls and are typically limited to seniors and executed in the spring after exams. However, Rene was quite insistent that she create one and not wait to execute it. Bringing attention to herself is not a quality I had associated with Rene in the past; therefore, I argue the public nature of this work holds meaning beyond execution for its own sake. I argue that Rene was now announcing to the school community this inner dialogue and struggle through visual signs. It is part of the work to be in public and viewed by others daily. Moreover, Rene assigns literal words to her feelings within this artwork, making them available for all viewers. I argue that this public display is another form of Rene constructing her identity and understanding of her sense of self within the school community. She has moved from sharing her experiences with just me (or a select few) to introducing her "self" to the school community through a semiotic lens.

Figures 6.5 and 6.6 are about communicating or expressing to others her traumatic past experiences and the intertwining affective elements of them. More importantly Rene intentionally used the art process as the vehicle to navigate her liminal experience. This is supported by her conscious use of the art and its presentation to engage others in a semiotic dialogue and the sudden use of linguistic signs when she previously was incapable of employing them.

The sculpture in Figure 6.5 consists of a found object door (an actual door) painted white with a plaster casting of Rene's (actual) hand in place of the doorknob. "Well, I started working in sculpture because I felt like I needed to put a piece of me in it" (Rene). It is significant to highlight the choice to literally incorporate an aspect of her body and by her own words "me" in the sculpture. She discusses how this piece is about the idea of becoming more open or presumably emotionally accessible, which suggests transformation (Mezirow, 2000). It is worth noting a similarity to the previous painting (Figure 6.1) that represents the figure waving. In this sculpture a cast of Rene's hand is placed where a doorknob would traditionally be located. The cast of the hand must be

FIGURE 6.5 Found object sculpture that uses an actual door with a cast of Rene's hand in place of the door knob

grabbed like in a handshake in order to open the door. Like waving in the previous piece (Figure 6.1), this is a form of greeting but it can occur in the three-dimensional world and one can literally grasp a cast of her hand. Rene explains:

> A lot of times you have to have someone ask you to open up. So, this door is just sort of, like, this barrier between what's in my mind, what I'm thinking and the outside world. And the hand is really me reaching out to sort of sitting there waiting for someone to grab it and then open up the door to see what's inside. (Rene)

The use of a cast of her own hand is an interesting and important element in Rene's liminal journey. In the first piece (Figure 6.1), the symbol or sign of the hand held implicit relevance to issues of power, which was supported by the overt reference to abuse. However, in this piece Rene creates a cast of her hand to function as a mechanism for opening a literal door. I argue that within this piece the issues relating to power have changed or altered. It is important to note that this piece was created following the completion of the public mural, which I argue was a public discourse with the school community. The hand in this piece has literal form and physical existence, as well as being extended. The extension of a hand is by tradition a willing and confident act. One grips someone else's hand and Rene stated that the hand is waiting for someone to engage with her and ask her to open up. Therefore, the extension of the hand is an invitation on her part.

Rene, as compared to Aline and Jayden, makes the most overt representations of the emotional and psychological act of crossing thresholds. In this piece, the symbol of the door is clearly claimed as an intended meaning of the piece. Rene frames the opening of doors as someone "looking in" with the implication of one accessing her feelings and experiences, which is indicative of the transformative experience (Mezirow, 2000). However, a door swings in both directions, which means that Rene can walk out of her current space and into a new space.

It is important to think of the door in the context of linguistic signs which have been an integral concern in Rene's liminal journey. More specifically, Rene has used the artwork as an intentional means of engaging others in conversation. This, in my case, was a literal conversation. As previously described, Rene created the door piece as an intended concrete representation of a more accessible self to others. However, dialogue is clearly important to Rene and, therefore, seeing the piece as allowing one access to her true self is a limited understanding of the work and her liminal journey. The accessing of one's self clearly occurs through relationships and dialogue and, I would argue, it is not just to allow one to see in – in this case what is needed is for Rene to step out. In other words, the reality of linguistic signs, for Rene, is one of establishing power over the affective element of her liminal state. The dialogic element (whether visual or linguistic) consistently provides a form of empowerment over her past trauma and an acceptance of self.

Therefore, the symbol of the door and the cast hand are more than coincidence. They are a form of tacit understanding of the liminal state through an affective lens. Moreover, it is the dialogic element of visual and linguistic signs that empower Rene's ability to navigate liminality. The increasing ability, value, and representations of linguistic signs is arguably evidence of Rene moving through the liminal space and crossing thresholds. The use of the door and the hand are powerful symbols of this journey. Although Rene does not possess academic awareness of threshold theory, her affective experience is arguably the most authentic experience with threshold crossing. I argue Rene demonstrates this understanding in her artwork.

Figure 6.6 is another sculpture and it consists of two hands. The lower hand that is reaching upward and is colored with yellow and red paint, represents Rene's hand. She states: "Only one of the hands is mine. The one down here. I purposely did this because this one represents myself and it's sort of reaching out to this other hand." Rene specifically identifies the second hand as female: "And this one's supposed to represent something pure. [...] I tried to go for sort

FIGURE 6.6
A sculpture of two hands reaching toward each other. The lower hand is wounded and reaching for help while the upper hand is reaching down

of a feminine feel, especially because a lot of times women are considered to be more caring and nurturing." Rene explains that the lower hand that represents her is colored in order to represent blood and that it is broken. "It needs nurturing. So, it's reaching out to the other hand and just trying to say, "I want help." Rene presents the artwork as reaching out to another, which is obviously an element of her story and the sculpture. However, she acknowledged that the hands could represent a dialogue within the self between her more broken self and a stronger and more pure side.

Figure 6.7 shows examples of Rene's photography, which is a medium she began to work in due to a dissatisfaction with sculpture. According to Rene, sculpture has "distortions of material" that she felt distracted the viewer from the intention and meaning of the piece. I argue this point of view is worth some discussion because I believe Rene is not articulating what she truly means. According to Rene, photography "really captures – you can really tell who it is." She believes the photographs are meant to capture varied feelings she has about herself in relation to her experiences. In my view, the most

FIGURE 6.7   Digital photograhs of Rene meant to capture her feelings about her sense of self

important aspect of photography, for Rene, is that it captures her likeness (as she stated in the previous quote). The argument I am making is the previous sculptures and painting were visual representations of her shifting ontological state as she began to navigate the affective elements of the liminal state. As discussed above, the previous artwork demonstrates an evolving shift into three-dimensional form and visual presentation that invited viewers to engage with her feelings and experiences. Therefore, the use of her likeness, captured in photography, is another ontological shift that implies aspects of crossing a threshold of acceptance and healing of self.

More specifically, Rene often discusses feelings of shame in relation to her past and the difficulty this had on her ability to form linguistic signs and discuss her feelings. It is important to highlight that her work increasingly involved aspects of inviting the viewer to engage with her on an intimate and personal level. I argue this effort to consider the viewer was one element of her liminal journey. Furthermore, Rene described her final sculpture (Figure 6.6) as a dialogue between her broken and stronger self, which I argue is indicative of an acceptance of self. Therefore, the use of her photographic likeness is a logical and important continuation of her liminal journey. I argue that in order to use her likeness, Rene must have overcome (to some degree) her feelings of shame and guilt that had been an affective element of her liminal state for many years. I also argue that Rene's original statements about photography removing distortions of material is a misrepresentation of her true meaning. The use of her photographic likeness is another important evolution in her liminal journey that suggests a more holistic representation of her ontological state of self-acceptance.

3 Rene and the Navigation of the Liminal Space and Threshold Crossing

This chapter focusing on Rene and her experiences highlights thresholds and associated liminality of self-regarding issues of healing and acceptance. There is a clear and profound intertwining with the affective dimension (Land et al., 2014; Land, 2014) and I argue there was more initial awareness regarding the cognitive dimension in the case of Rene. In other words, Rene clearly understood her past experiences and the impact of feelings of shame and guilt which resulted in an inability to talk about her past. More importantly, Rene had the cognitive awareness to identify her feelings as well as their origin. I think this is an important distinction from Aline and Jayden in that Rene did not necessarily formulate the cognitive awareness or thoughts as a result of art making. Rather, the affective nature of her experiences arguably acted as an obstacle or weight that prevented Rene from articulating thoughts to others as well as an inability to integrate or accept these experiences and reconcile the ongoing troublesomeness.

Troublesomeness that involves conflict of the cognitive and affective dimension, in the context of transformation, is addressed in the threshold literature. More specifically, Timmermans (2010) points out that some individuals remain in a stuck place while others open up. The implication is that the affective complexity (Land et al., 2014) impedes the cognitive development as well. Timmermans (2010) further argues that the epistemic potential of individuals may become relevant in reference to the zone of proximal development (Vygotsky, 1978), more specifically, to aspects of knowledge construction that individuals can achieve alone as compared to aspects of knowledge construction in which individuals need assistance. Maturity and individual context are clearly relevant factors in such transformations as well as psychological attributes (Land et al., 2014); however, the epistemic elements of visual art possess unique qualities regarding the formation of meaning. As discussed in the previous section, Rene's artwork functioned as a means for her to engage with others and convey meaning in a manner she felt was safe for her to do so. Furthermore, the evolving portfolio empowered shifts in ontological states that allowed Rene to engage in self-dialogue that resulted in a more holistic understanding and acceptance of self. I argue that the vehicle of visual art empowered Rene to navigate the affective elements of the liminal space as a semiotic vehicle for the making of meaning and dialogue.

When one considers Rene's portfolio and her explanation of the art pieces, she consistently represents the self as being introduced or accessed by the world. When considered in the theoretical context of thirdness (Bhabha, 1990) and socialization, the self is (in part) directly shaped by interactions with others. In Rene's case it can be argued that the truth of her prior experiences and their impact were inaccessible to others and her internal self arguably was less evolved. However, her external identity would be understood and recognized by many.

Rene is explicit in the power of the affective dimension in her experience with liminality. She discusses her inability to form or at least voice linguistic signs due to the overwhelming emotional connotations inherent within them. Rene also presents as an individual who is well aligned to the research of Land, Rattray, and Vivian (2014) in that she has certain attributes that allow for hope or efficacy. According to the research, this likely empowered her ability to move on. It is interesting that she quickly understood visual art in a semiotic theoretical context and consciously employed this understanding to give voice to her struggle. As a result, the visual arts became a vehicle for traversing the liminal state.

4 Semiotic Dialogue: Communication, Expression, and Voice

In my view, a remarkable aspect of Rene's case is the intentional use of the dialogic element of the visual art-making process. More specifically, the dialogic element is crucial in the navigation of the liminal space, threshold crossing, and in the overcoming of the affective barriers. Meyer and Land (2003) identify the dialogic element of threshold crossing as a change in language that is indicative of a new understanding of a field and identity in a community of practice. In the context of this study and especially in the case of Rene, the dialogic element functions as a semiotic discourse with others. I argue that the visual art-making process provided semiotic discourse with others that, in turn, supported her evolution into an understanding of self. In other words, Rene continually used visual art as a semiotic discourse to introduce and form a sense of self within the community. Her artwork was a means of holding conversations and processing her trauma despite the overpowering impact of the affective dimension. As Rene continually stated, she knew the words or thoughts she wanted to convey but was incapable of speaking them. The dialogic element expressed through visual signs allow Rene to further develop her sense of self.

Arguably, Rene more consciously understands the visual arts through a semiotic lens. As previously mentioned, Rene made a conscious decision and effort to entice me to inquire about her past trauma using visual signs. Rene is in somewhat of a contrast to Jayden and Aline in that there is a cognitive awareness of this dialogic element. Jayden and Aline, however, engaged in a more tacit process at first and awareness evolved as they understood their work with more depth and clarity.

When considered in a succession of work, Figure 6.1 (the handprint piece) suggests the origins of forming a self or perhaps a glimpse of a complex threshold of self. More specifically, the artwork visually represents a feeling of being in flux and the figure is either emerging from a precipice of a tunnel or is in danger of falling into an abyss. The mural is suggestive of being a part of the world or an entity within it as Rene creates visual signs and uses linguistic signs to engage public viewers in a dialogue. Moreover, the door piece suggests physical form and structure that is dimensional and is presented in time and space. When considering the ephemeral quality of Figure 6.1, the permanence and physicality of this work is an important contrast. The act of making it real suggests a further movement through the liminal space. The viewer is invited to grasp the hand and interact with the work, opening the door if they choose, which is a profound change from the earlier use of the hand in reference to power and abuse. The implication is that Rene is constructing access to the world or a new space and that she has control or power manifest in her invitation to grasp her hand.

Finally, Rene employed photography to represent her literal image without what she called the distortions of material. As previously stated, the photos are not particularly strong artwork, but they are significant in how she describes the need for a true image of her. In other words, this transition observed through her portfolio is indicative of the formation of a self. The use of the materials and how her ideas were represented and presented to viewers continually involved a dialogic element through the semiotic lens. It was through this dialogue that Rene could navigate the associated liminality of self and arguably cross the complex threshold.

The intuitive ability of Rene to grasp and employ the dialogic aspect of visual art is not only impressive but an essential role in her navigation of the liminal space. In other words, the semiotic conversations with viewers offers an empowerment which is like Aline's experience of exhibiting her work in the gallery. An important distinction is that, for Aline, the literal interactions and validation from viewers about her work and bravery provided a healing experience. In the case of Rene, the validation is not a direct experience but a form of empowerment. In my view, the act of making the work and having it viewed in public is enough and the empowerment is found in Rene having voice or giving voice to her troublesome past. In this specific context, Rene shares the details of her past, but it seems this is kept for relationships she values. Therefore, the experience of presenting her voice in a public manner or giving form and name to her underlying troublesomeness empowers her to accept the self in a manner she had struggled with for a long time.

When I contacted Rene to ask her permission to use her images and story for this book, we had spent time catching up. She has successfully completed an undergraduate program in a field in which she holds passion. Rene also told me she is engaged to be married which I hope is an indication that she has been able to form healthy and loving relationships.

References

Bhabha, H. (1990). The third space: Interview with Homi Bhabha. In J. Rutherford (Ed.), *Identity: Community, culture, difference* (pp. 207–221). Lawrence & Wishart.

Land, R. (2014, July). *Liminality close-up* [Paper presentation]. HECU7 at Lancaster University.

Land, R., Rattray, J., & Vivian, P. (2014). Learning in the liminal space: A semiotic approach to threshold concepts. *Higher Education, 67*(2), 199–217.

Langer, S. K. (1942). *Philosophy in a new key: A study in the symbolism of reason, rite and art*. Harvard University Press.

Mezirow, J. (2000). Learning to think like an adult: Core concepts of transformation theory. In J. Mezirow & Associates (Eds.), *Learning as transformation: Critical perspectives on a theory in progress* (pp. 3–33). Jossey-Bass.

Timmermans, J. A. (2010). Changing our minds: The developmental potential of threshold concepts. In J. H. F. Meyer, R. Land, & C. Baillie (Eds.), *Threshold concepts and transformational learning* (pp. 3–19). Sense.

Vygotsky, L. (1978). Interaction between learning and development. *Readings on the Development of Children*, 23(3), 34–41.

CHAPTER 7

Cade: "Because I Don't Care What You Think"

1   Introduction

Cade was 18 years old at the time he made the presented art portfolio and he was in college when I asked him if I could include him in this book. Cade is a homosexual male and I worked with him for all four years of his secondary education. Cade's personal and artistic journey explores the visual art-making process as a semiotic navigation of self and the development of a voice. During his high school career Cade had evolved into a confident young man whom any parent would be proud to call their son. In middle and early high school, Cade struggled with understanding and coming to terms with his sexual orientation. In his junior year, Cade had "come out" without apology to anyone. He discussed his sexual orientation with his parents and one close friend when he came out, but his view was that the rest of the world could take it or leave it. Presumably, most teachers make mental observations about students and I had suspected at times that Cade was gay. However, my formal introduction to the Cade that was "out" resulted from me asking about prom; he responded that he was going with his boyfriend. This was his first public acknowledgement (in my presence and in a class full of students) about his orientation. His artwork during this period was indicative of personal struggle and dark emotions, which indicates Cade had struggled with the reality of being gay. According to Cade, his struggle was not the behavior of being gay but the issues of identity and self. However, Cade had suddenly embraced the whole of his identity and his artwork addressed issues relating to self and voice.

As has been indicated in the previous case studies, "self" can be a complex threshold. In the context of Cade there is profound involvement of the affective element of self in coming to terms with a reality of self that deviates from the typical. Cade seems to have always understood that he was gay, but he had difficulty coming to terms with accepting his self and being out. His artwork documents this journey of not only accepting himself as a homosexual male but also becoming confident in who he is as an individual and developing what he calls his voice. There is a clear ontological shift in Cade which is found not only in his acceptance of himself as a homosexual male but in his ability to align his inner experience of self with the more external and socially constructed identity. This acceptance of one's self is indicative of the transformative aspect of threshold crossing as a significant shift in the perception

© KONINKLIJKE BRILL NV, LEIDEN, 2022 | DOI:10.1163/9789004508132_007

of personal identity, a reconstruction of subjectivity (Meyer & Land, 2006). Although Cade has experienced this transformation, there were many years in which he struggled and shifted between accepting himself as a homosexual and not. The affective element is clearly inherent in the liminal experience (i.e., Land, 2014; Rattray, 2016; Meyer & Land, 2006) and impacted his the ability to navigate the liminal space. There is an interesting interrelationship when considering the self as a complex threshold with liminality navigated through visual art. The subjective nature of the creative process, visual language, and expressed meaning is a unique manner with which to observe and further conceptualize the complexity of self.

It is important to note that I was Cade's teacher for multiple years, and I have the benefit of an established relationship that holds enough trust so that he is willing to participate as a case study in this research. I would imagine most educators encounter students who are struggling or open with issues of sexuality and have supported those students in various ways. My point is that this level of confidence and trust, which is a necessary element for a student to engage in such a vulnerable process, has developed over time. Although Cade's journey involves a struggle with self through his sexuality, the more relevant aspect is the role of his art-making process in the navigation of his liminal journey.

2   Identity and Self

In Chapter 1, I established the importance of the constructs of self and identity. These constructs were integral to each of the case studies thus far as complex threshold concepts that each of the young people navigate. However, due to the involvement of sexual orientation with Cade and his struggle with "coming out" I am going to address the issue further in the context of Cade's experiences.

"A central task of adolescent development is the formation of an identity" (Degges-White & Myers, 2005, p. 186). "The formation of identity required to synthesize childhood identifications in such a way that he can both establish a reciprocal relationship with his society and maintain a feeling of continuity within himself " (Marcia, 1966, p. 551). Erikson (1968) and Marcia (1966) refer to the young adult becoming a participating member of society as a citizen and through their occupation. Fearon (1999, p. 23) conceives of "personal identity as consisting of aspects of themselves that they feel powerless to change, or which in their experience they cannot choose, such as sexual orientation or membership in a social category." The common ground among these conceptualizations is the role of social construction and the relevance of the perception of others.

There are many facets to academic understanding of the constructs of self and identity (Waterman, 1999; Van Hoof, 1997), some of which can be attributed to evolving understandings associated with changing society and the consciousness of individuals. This evolving understanding, in my experience, has been evident in recent years as individuals have become more open about sexual orientation and issues of transgender. Identity politics of gender, sexuality, and race contributes to changing conceptualizations of the construct of self and identity (Fearon, 1999; Waterman, 1999; Van Hoof, 1997). In the context of Cade's experiences, there is an important distinction between identity and internal feelings about the self (Fearon, 1999). "There can be no argument but that the subjective feeling state of having a self is an important empirical phenomenon that warrants study in its own right" (Epstein, 1973, p. 2).

In the relation to Cade's experiences, these distinctions are more than academic. Integral to the struggle of sexual orientation is the element of perception by others about a lifestyle and one's response to that. There is also one's internal feelings about homosexuality. Clearly, the overlap of identity and self are complex; one can have internal feelings about how others perceive their identity and one can also struggle with internal feelings of being gay. Clearly, the involvement of affect is inextricable in the stages of identity formation in this context. The community and family within which an individual is born and socialized can have a profound impact on one's ability to navigate such identity complexities. Cade must navigate the perceptions others may hold toward the homosexual community despite his individual characteristics. In other words, Cade may not always be perceived as an individual who happens to be gay. In situations of intolerance or hatred, Cade can be perceived as a bad or evil person simply because of his shared characteristics with a larger subset of people; this more public perception was a concern to Cade. Furthermore, Cade has also struggled with his own sense of self as a homosexual, which had an impact on his willingness to be out.

Identity synthesis is an important and final stage of homosexual identity formation. As one evolves to this final of five stages, one has full acceptance of their homosexual identity (Cass, 1984). The distinction of the identity synthesis phase is "private and public sexual identities become synthesized into one image of self" (Cass, 1984, p. 234). However, the implied sense of wholeness is not exclusive to an ideal homosexual identity formation. "Its most obvious concomitants are a feeling of being at home in one's body" (Erikson, 1968, p. 165) and a feeling of confidence and assuredness in a mutual recognition by important individuals.

The relevance of this section is to conceptualize key concepts of the case study as well as to highlight the significance of the self in Cade's liminal journey and establish conceptual grounding for understanding self as a threshold.

Cade discusses his struggle with elements of self as opposed to the general label of "gay." I asked Cade the meaning of the constructs of identity and self:

> I feel like self and identity are really closely related. I feel like self is something you need to be comfortable with, and not what others are. Then, I feel like identity is maybe how others see you more. You are this identity. That's how other people identify you. I'm using kind of the word and the definition there. Then self is kind of everything that makes you. That is, that you're made of. Everything that you're made of and kind of how you see yourself. How you perceive others to see yourself. (Cade)

I am not interested in contributing to any refinement of academic discussions of the meaning of identity or self nor to a deeper understanding of homosexual identity. In my view, the context of threshold concepts dictates the constructs of identity and self should be approached, as a means, to glimpse the individual experiencing within. I acknowledge that sexual orientation and gender issues are complex aspects of identity formation and as an art educator I have empathy and compassion for these various experiences. The issue for this case study of Cade is the internal experience of self in relationship to this more public presentation of identity, or what is called identity synthesis (Cass, 1984).

3 Crisis and Troublesome Knowledge

Much of the literature on identity formation discusses the role of crisis (i.e., Erikson, 1968; Marcia, 1966; Cass, 1979). For example, the constructs identity achievement and identity foreclosed reference individuals who have committed to an identity with or without facing crisis (Marcia, 1966). "Without having faced crisis point or having had exposure to identity possibilities, they have prematurely committed to a particular identity choice" (Degges-White & Myers, 2005, p. 187). The implication is that crisis is ultimately a positive contribution to identity formation. Erikson (1968, p. 163) states that "normative crisis is a normal phase of increased ego strength. [...] [It] revives dormant anxiety and arouses new conflict, but also supports expanded ego function in the searching and playful engagement of new opportunities and associations."

There is a direct relationship between the concept of crisis and that of disequilibrium (Piaget, 1976) and troublesome knowledge when considered in the context of the self as a threshold. There are also parallels between stuck place and the liminal space with constructs, such as identity moratorium (Marcia, 1966; Degges-White & Myers, 2005). More specifically, identity moratorium is experienced by an individual who has faced crisis but still has not committed to an identity (Marcia, 1966; Degges-White & Myers, 2005). I argue that the affective element of the liminal state is relevant and a linking concept to identity-formation theories. "During the final stage of his identity formation, [a person] is apt to suffer more deeply than [they] ever did before or ever will again from a confusion of roles" (Erikson, 1968, p. 163).

Cass (1979) presents an identity-formation theory specific to homosexuality. Inherent in this process of identity formation is an incongruency of perception of self, as well as a concern over others' perception of the individual (Cass, 1979). "It is probably impossible [...] to achieve a homosexual defining matrix that is totally (cognitively and affectively) congruent. It is possible, however, for incongruency to be reduced to a level that is tolerable and manageable" (Cass, 1979, p. 222).

Obviously, research that has built upon the seminal work (Cass, 1979) has demonstrated the profoundly troublesome nature of homosexual identity formation. In the context of Cade's experiences, he initially struggled with accepting the reality of his orientation and underwent a process of denial. However, the aspect of societal pressure played a part in this initial struggle and continued to be of concern in his coming-out process. These aspects of identity formation are addressed within this chapter and the interviews with Cade. There is much evidence of increased bullying, suicide, and mental health issues related to homosexual youth, particularly as they come out. The point I am trying to explicate is the relatively understood reality of homosexual youth considered in the context of crisis in identity formation with the intent of highlighting the increased intensity of the difficult experience. The following section presents an account of Cade acknowledging and coming to terms with his sexual orientation. This account by Cade is a reflective process which provides a basis of understanding Cade's development through the art-making process. Moreover, Cade presents his experience as relatively positive, but the troublesome nature of the affective involvement is profound, despite the supportive environment in which Cade exists. More specifically, Cade initially struggles with accepting his homosexual desires and attempts to deny them, thinking that they are "bad" or "wrong." This, in turn, impacts his cognitive processes and informs perspective and ensuing behavior that is consistent with his internal feelings.

4   Cade: "Because I Feel Like the Voice Is Definitely a Big Part of Myself and Who I Am"

As previously mentioned, I have worked with Cade since he was in ninth grade, which has afforded me the opportunity to form a valued relationship with a wonderful young man. Cade is sensitive and private, causing him to often edit his words. In each year of his high school career there were significant changes to Cade's work. These changes to his visual artwork document his liminal journey and, as evidenced in his portfolio, functions as a semiotic discourse with the self. Cade's journey of accepting his homosexuality and feeling empowered to come out constitutes his liminal journey and threshold crossing. His final IB exhibition provides clear evidence of the ontological shift that is further supported by his exhibition text, which articulates a clarity and intentional use of signs and symbols that are expressive of his felt experience.

"Well, when I first started having these kinds of different feelings and stuff like that, I would of course explore upon them as anyone else would" (Cade). The implication is that Cade developed romantic and physical desire for other young men and had explored these feelings in a typical adolescent manner. The importance of this point is the suggestion that Cade did not struggle with the physical and sexual aspects of homosexuality but did struggle with issues related to self and identity.

> Then, it got to this point where I felt it was wrong myself. I would deny it every time this kind of feeling came up or anything like that. I would deny that part of myself and say, "It's just a phase." I'm going to move on from it. Don't act upon it and don't do anything. It's not for real. It's not going to last. (Cade)

According to Cade, this emotional and psychological struggle lasted for several years (seventh grade to tenth grade), which is a distinct struggle from the issue of "coming out." Cade is referring to the struggle for internal acknowledgement (or acceptance) that he is gay, which he makes prolonged attempts to resist and deny.

> I didn't like that part of myself when I was that age. Like I said, I kept it under wraps. I tried to hide it away from myself. I told myself that it wasn't really me. Then [there's] society, [and] you read. You see all these things about how that community of people can get so much hate. [...] But that was always [what] I was so afraid of. Even if I am this way, could I be accepted? Would I be safe in this world? (Cade)

There is a transition being presented through a process of reflection, in the interview, which points to issues of identity and self. Cade describes an ability at some point to internally acknowledge that he is gay but the idea of being "out" was frightening to him; there was a lack of confidence in feeling physically,

FIGURE 7.1
Installation created by Cade during his freshman year of high school and incorporated his body

psychologically, and emotionally safe. In other words, Cade is reflecting upon an inability to be ok with feelings about the self that being "out" would present to the world. Obviously, these are valid concerns over how the world would respond to him, even though our school and surrounding community is relatively progressive in social views.

Cade describes his sophomore year as one where he began to acknowledge that the feelings he was experiencing were more than just a phase:

> Then, when I met the person, the man who I'm dating now, I kind of didn't care about what the world would kind of think or anything like that. I know my friends would still support me. I know my family would still support me. [...] They didn't know. But just the way that they have acted. I know that they would love me unconditionally. I know that even if the world doesn't like me, I know that these people still will. (Cade)

There is a nice romantic notion to Cade's finding of confidence that holds roots in the internal acknowledgement of being gay. Knowing Cade, as I do, I argue he has possessed an integrity and strength all along that found empowerment in the support of others. As he stated, he knew the people closest to him would support him and his newly found relationship clearly influenced this strength. "At that point, I kind of started to let my guard down. Then, as I have been going through the past two years with this, it has definitely gotten a lot better" (Cade).

Cade made the decision to "come out" to his parents (who were already divorced at the time) and his best friend, who happened to be female. In the interview he gives an account of the reactions of the chosen individuals. He describes catching each of his parents by surprise. Meaning, they did not suspect he was gay. He describes their reaction as shocked but loving and supportive. His father's reaction was troubling in Cade's view, because he suggested that Cade not date until he was out of high school. Cade interprets this as a suggestion informed by love and concern that he may be subject to bullying. However, Cade did take exception to the comment but did not express his views to his father. Overall, Cade perceives the experience with his parents as positive and he maintains a normal relationship with them to this day. His best friend reacted with a positive "squeal" and a hug, which suggests she had suspected all along he was gay. As mentioned in the introduction, Cade is a private person so he only "came out" to these three people and everyone else basically discovered it on their own. From the outside looking in, one simply discovered one day that Cade was openly gay.

It is important to highlight that Cade caught his parents by surprise and his mother responded that she loves, him, but she would have to adjust because no parent would want this for their child. Cade interprets this as a concern for his safety or empathy for the associated struggles. Considering these experiences in the context of identity and self, Cade had to first accept and understand these feelings within himself and experience a reconfiguring on his own. A further complexity is that Cade had to reintroduce himself to people who know him intimately and, in this case, it was a different and unexpected identity which is part of their perception. This, in turn, must have an impact on the affective levels of self.

Despite the seemingly abrupt transition, Cade clearly struggled for years with accepting the reality of his sexual orientation. Even after his "coming out," Cade did not necessarily editorialize his orientation. Issues of self and feeling comfortable within oneself and relationships to identity within society influence Cade. There are also personal attributes that impact upon these issues as well. As mentioned in the introduction, Cade is shy and introverted. When struggles with identity and orientation were encountered as troublesome knowledge, he experienced self-hatred and a rejection of the self. As a result, he isolated himself from others.

> I was only close with a couple of people. I was very shy. People just kind of scared me in general. It was thanks to you that I kind of branched out into talking to more people. I remember. You would look at my art and be, like, "What is this about?" I would either say nothing. Or, I'd say like two words. [...] You would try to get me to explain. Then, you would push me to try other art forms, and just kind of push me out there. It was the combination of you, and then my friends, and having to make new friends. It was the combination of all those kinds of things that kind of pushed me to find different things and explore upon those different things. That kind of made up of myself that I maybe didn't notice at first. It was kind of deep down in there. (Cade)

122   CHAPTER 7

The implication of this excerpt is the role of visual art as a semiotic discourse
that results in an ability to engage with and understand the self. This specific
time period was during Cade's freshman year and he created an installation
(Figure 7.1) that was based on a drawing he did. The artworks suggested a
young man who was feeling trapped and engaged in a struggle.

This section presented Cade's experiences with recognizing and accepting
his sexual orientation, including his struggle with his internal self and more
external identity. The next section introduces Cade's art portfolio, which documents his resubjectivity and the role of art making as an element in this
journey. We gain more insight into Cade's felt experience and a depth of understanding (Leavy, 2015; Eisner, 2008; Barone & Eisner, 1997).

5   Cade's Art Portfolio

The following statement was submitted by Cade, along with his art portfolio,
for external assessment during his senior year. The statement is a description
of the intention of his artwork as well as curatorial approaches to how he set
up his exhibition.

> For my exhibition, I have created several pieces that relate to my central
> concept of "self-censored." This phrase is the driving force behind every
> one of my pieces. It is representative of the way I have felt since a young
> age, not being able to speak my mind and use my voice. I have always felt
> like I had to keep my emotions and opinions to myself, censoring what
> I should and shouldn't say and feel. I have set up my work in a way that
> represents my evolution of self during my years in high school. The first
> piece I had recreated from my freshman year installation is the "creeping
> shadows" which starts in the corner of the gallery, which is why I have
> chosen to exhibit here. When I had created the original piece, I was strug-
> gling with my own identity and found myself trapped by the inability to
> accept what I had been feeling. I was trapped within myself, much like the
> shadows cornering my emotions and holding them there. The shadows of
> the installation are also shown branching away from the corner toward
> my other pieces. As the years past I continued to become more accept-
> ing of who I am and who I was becoming. Therefore, there is a layer of
> pieces that represent my evolution. Two of my pieces in this show involve
> mouths, *Non-Verbal* and *Nevermind*, that represent my lack of voice. The
> large scale of my pieces illustrates the presence of these feelings within
> myself. The image of the bleeding gums represents the frustration I went

through in coming to terms with my emotions. And my final piece that I selected is the performance piece, *Breakthrough*. This last piece was selected to signify the end of my feeling of being trapped behind doors. I had come to terms with my identity and accepted who I am. This piece is displayed furthest away from the corner and close to an open window to show my distance from my previous feelings of being trapped. The door is a symbol of the threshold that I break through into a deeper acceptance of myself. The overt violence and destruction are symbolic of the catharsis involved as well as the emotional and psychological turmoil. My exhibition is representative of my evolution from my first years of high school and moving away from the corner and reaching self-acceptance.

The overall views of Cade's exhibition (Figure 7.2) give some insight into the visual language which Cade finds expressive in terms of design elements, form, and symbols. More importantly, the photographs provide visual evidence as to the narrative that underpins Cade's curatorial choices. More specifically, Cade chose to install his work in the triangular gallery space in the front of our school building. Cade's use of this space removed his work from the primary location where most student exhibitions were displayed. The relevance of this point is the use of the school gallery is not common nor prestigious in this context and, in my mind, indicates Cade's commitment to the intention of his work.

As the artist statement indicates, Cade recreated the installation he made in ninth grade (Figure 7.1) in the corner of the gallery as an origin to his artistic and liminal journeys. The rest of the exhibition uses more overt symbolism and is representative of the ontological shift experienced by Cade as he began to develop his voice and fully embrace it. "I was struggling with my own identity and found myself trapped by the inability to accept what I had been feeling. I was trapped within myself, much like the shadows cornering my emotions and holding them there" (Cade).

FIGURE 7.2   Overall views of Cade's final IB exhibition

FIGURE 7.3   Drawings made of marker on paper

It is important to consider these curatorial aspects along with Cade's choice of symbols – specifically, the repeated use of mouths and the overt destruction of a door. It is clear that Cade is representing his experience of engaging with the troublesome feelings associated with his homosexuality. These affective elements created conflict in Cade's more internal experience of self as well as his willingness to allow homosexuality to become a more overt aspect of his public and socially constructed identity. Implicit in Cade's account is the argument that the affective elements associated with Cade's struggle for identity formation lacked the ability to navigate the associated liminal space. With this overview in mind, the rest of this section addresses the individual pieces that comprise Cade's art portfolio.

These graphic artworks (Figure 7.3) were not included in Cade's final portfolio for submission. However, it is important to include these images because they represent a sudden and radical change in Cade's artwork that became more explicit and confrontational. More specifically, these images are very bold in color and design with a graphic style which confronts the viewer's eye and commands attention. Based upon the brief descriptions provided about Cade and his struggles, I think it is clear this type of visual work was not typical of Cade up to this point. In his previous work the expressive intention was often diluted and lacked the potency of the work you see in his portfolio.

Cade had begun making this work after he had come out and began dating his boyfriend. I argue that these images document a change or movement within the liminal space for Cade in the sense the work expresses, in a bold way, how he had been feeling and possibly still feeling about his homosexual identity. In other words, by coming out and dating he had, in part, stopped "censoring" himself, but the boldness of the images suggests an intensity of feeling which may still have been felt at this time.

Creeping Shadows (Figure 7.4) is the re-creation of installation Cade had made in ninth grade (Figure 7.1). The installation is made of cut paper and "the

FIGURE 7.4
"Creeping Shadows" is made of cut paper and is reminiscent of the installation Cade created in ninth grade

piece deals with my suppressed feelings of depression and denial about my sexual orientation and my emotions of feeling trapped in my identity" (Cade). This piece evolved from being a drawing in his sketchbook to becoming a larger scale installation. In my experience, not many 14-year-old students have the expressive ambition to translate a drawing into an installation. At the time of the initial drawing and first installation, Cade had already been struggling with his sexuality, but he had not realized that his felt experience was being represented in his artwork. It is important to consider the effort and commitment required of Cade to create the installation, which suggests the art-making experience was expressive or meaningful in some way to him. I argue this is indicative of the willingness to reduce the affective aspect of the liminal space through experimentation with artwork (Land, 2014). As Cade reflects upon that installation, he suggests that it was his first artwork that expressed his experiences with sexuality. The re-creation of the artwork suggests that Cade viewed this piece as his first artwork that engages and expresses his struggles and navigation of the liminal state.

Non-Verbal (Figure 7.5) is a sculpture made of a wire armature that was then covered with plaster; the letters are cardboard, which were also covered in plaster in order to unify the surface of the sculpture. Once the sculpture was sanded and refined it was then painted with acrylic paints. "This piece follows along with the concept of self-censored as the words are coming out of the mouth but are stuck to the tongue. It is representative of all the words and phrases I always felt like I had to censor and keep to myself" (Cade).

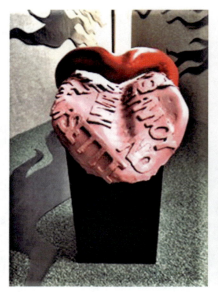 

FIGURE 7.5   "Non Verbal" is a plaster sculpture that depicts a mouth with words on the tongue

The use of the mouth is obviously important and is intended to represent his inability to form linguistic signs. I use this phrase because of the way Cade articulates the meaning of the work by saying the words were stuck on his tongue, even though he felt he had to keep them to himself. The point being made is that the words being stuck suggests more than a self-censoring and almost literally references the construct of the stuck place (to which Cade was never introduced). The implication points to the affective element of his liminal experience in combination with discursive elements of threshold crossing. More specifically, the affect involved in Cade's liminal experience is obviously profound and impacting his ability to engage with the associated feelings and construct meaning. In the context of the discursive elements, the idea of words being stuck on the tongue suggest that they were not fully or coherently formed. I would argue that if this piece were completely about self-censoring or editing, the imagery would likely suggest or involve swallowing words or sewing a mouth shut. The sculpture being called *Non-Verbal* suggests an inability to speak as opposed to choosing not to speak.

The use of the mouth form and the tongue sticking out is also a bold and evocative gesture, which, when considered with the previous discussion (Figure 7.3), becomes important. The *Self-Censor* pieces and *Non-Verbal* share a boldness of color, gesture, and graphic style. The sculpture commands attention and is juxtaposed with the idea of words not being fully formed or articulated.

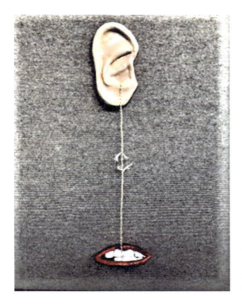

FIGURE 7.6
"Snap" is comprised of a mouth and ear made of ceramic clay that are connected by twine that is frayed

Snap is a ceramic sculpture that:

> has two parts held together by a string, which implies its fraying. The mouth that is hanging from the ear is not only closed but clenched shut. The fraying string and implied tension implies the closed mouth is going to drop and smash. The making of this piece has fostered my ability to understand myself and find voice. (Cade)

The presence of the word "understand" in Cade's description, along with the symbols of ear and clinched mouth, are, in my opinion, important semiotic signs. The mouth has a more active role of being clinched with the implication the mouth will shatter if it lets go of the string. This active clinching in conjunction with being suspended from the ear is more suggestive of the self-censorship to which Cade has consistently referred. The ear and the use of the word "understand" imply the presence of a cognitive element that was previously absent from Cade's visual language. When considered with the clinched mouth, I argue that the work suggests more of a conscious choice to not articulate his thoughts or feelings as opposed to not being able to form relevant linguistic signs. In turn, this points to the continual impact of the affective dimension in Cade's liminal experience in the sense that the clinched mouth is a choice by Cade and the implied danger is arguably perceived through the lens of this affective impact.

FIGURE 7.7
"Held In" is acrylic on two pieces of canvas that comprise the shape of a mouth

Held In (Figure 7.7) is a 6" × 11" acrylic painting on two pieces of canvas:

> This large piece expresses the underpinning pain associated with my lack of voice. The increased scale is intended to highlight the threshold of frustration and anger living in a societal reality where some perspectives are limited in their own opposition to that of the norm. This piece is representational of the transition from who I was, holding everything in and keeping it down, to who I am now. (Cade)

This artwork is arguably evidence of continual navigation of the liminal space in that it is a clear progression from the previous piece, *Snap*. There is great significance in the work being two pieces of canvas with a gap in between them and the use of the word "transition," which I argue is evidence of an ontological shift. Metaphorically, Cade has stopped clinching his mouth shut and has now opened it up in order to ease his frustration and pain. The space in between the canvases was a choice by Cade in the sense he could have aligned them to appear as though they were one single sheet. Instead, he involves the gap, which disrupts the gesture of clinched mouth and deintensifies the underpinning anguish.

Breakthrough Performance was presented as an installation that included video documentation of the destruction of a door. Figure 7.8 shows the residual artifacts that were used in the performance. The performance involved a repeated series of actions where Cade would smash the door with the sledgehammer and then make a feeble attempt to patch over it or repair the damage with patching plaster. "This piece is the result of a performance piece. The hammer and plaster used in the video are displayed as well to highlight the conflicting aspects of my emotions fighting over my identity. The violence and overall destruction of the door represents the pain felt during this evolution and self conflict" (Cade).

FIGURE 7.8
"Breakthrough Performance" consists of the physical remnants and a video documentation of a performance piece in which Cade smashes a door and tries to repair it

FIGURE 7.9   Video still from "Breakthrough Performance" where Cade is hitting the door with a sledge hammer

The images in Figure 7.9 are film stills from the video that was presented with the residual artifacts in Figure 7.8. The door was intact at the beginning of the performance and I am not aware of how Cade determined the point at which to stop.

Cade has chosen to employ a different symbol than a mouth as well as the medium of performance. This fluid thought process and experimental nature considered in the context of the use of a semiotic sign of a door suggests the idea of threshold crossing and transformation. There was no discussion as to the use of the symbol of a door, meaning I did not suggest it or help him consider the available options. Cade asked me how he could get a door to use for an artwork and I gave him a spare one that I had leftover from some house renovations. It is also significant that Cade used the word "threshold" in previous descriptions of his work, but not in this case, where it would be a logical choice of words. The point being made is, in my view, the previous pieces were a navigation of the liminal space as he was glimpsing and approaching the threshold of self, while this piece suggests an actual threshold crossing. I point to the drastic changes in style, material, and media in the different phases of his evolution. There was an increased urgency and playfulness (ambition) in the creation of his work. Cade had always been extremely methodical and even lacking confidence in many ways, which caused his art-making process to be slow and tedious. As he created the works in this portfolio, which I argue documents his movement through the liminal space, his production, confidence, and desire to experiment increased rapidly. These attributes are consistent with the liminal experience (Land, 2014).

The aggression or violence associated with the performance piece, in my opinion, is a powerful visual representation of the affective involvement in Cade's liminal experience. His linguistic descriptions of his feelings about his struggle with self, identity, and sexuality are a bit diluted. The artwork presents a more honest articulation of his internal experience and struggle. In my mind, his destruction of the threshold is a departure from his struggle and is a fitting embrace of his transformed self.

6   **Cade's Liminal Experience and Discursive Elements**

Cade's artwork presents a paradoxical reality which suggests the transformative and discursive characteristics of liminality and threshold crossing. The transformative characteristic of liminality is discussed in association with individuals entering into communities of practice (Meyer & Land, 2005) and is evidenced in a change in an individual's language. I argue that in the context of Cade's art making, the dramatic changes in his visual language are evidence of his movement in communities of practice as well as movement through the liminal space and threshold crossing.

Although Cade, at the time of his interview, is not overly articulate in his linguistic descriptions of his work and experiences there is a clarity in is thinking that has evolved. The art-making process and his choices in artistic medium, material, and process are quite sophisticated and acted as semiotic signs that informed a dialogue within himself as well as with me. I argue his use of visual language provided a means for him to engage troublesome emotions associated with identity and self that empowered him to express and construct meaning. As a result, Cade glimpsed relevant thresholds and navigated the associated liminal space and transforming into a healthier and more whole self that he is more able to accept and synthesize.

About a year after Cade graduated, he came back to visit me from college, where he is currently an art major. He is openly gay on campus and is taking full advantage of the social and academic offerings of college life. Cade had said he felt less refined or technically skilled than many of his fellow art majors, but he is more evolved in his conceptual understanding of the art-making process and the language of art. As we caught up and he filled me in on the gossip of his social life, he got up to leave and said, "I have to show you something." He unbuttoned his shirt to show me his first tattoo; it is located on his chest over his heart (see Figure 7.7).

In my mind, this expressive act is evidence of Cade's evolution and transformation to fully accept himself as a gay male. Moreover, it demonstrated to me there is much more to learning in the arts than mastery of a curriculum. It is our obligation, as art educators, to fully exploit this potential.

References

Barone, T., & Eisner, E. (1997). Arts-based educational research. *Complementary Methods for Research in Education*, 2, 75–116.

Cass, V. C. (1979). Homosexuality identity formation: A theoretical model. *Journal of Homosexuality*, *4*(3), 219–235.

Cass, V. C. (1984). Homosexual identity formation: Testing a theoretical model. *Journal of Sex Research*, *20*(2), 143–167.

Degges-White, S. E., & Myers, J. E. (2005). The adolescent lesbian identity formation model: Implications for counseling. *Journal of Humanistic Counseling*, *44*(2), 185–197.

Eisner, E. (2008). Art and knowledge. In J. G. Knowles & A. L. Cole (Eds.), *Handbook of the arts in qualitative research: Perspectives, methodologies, examples, and issues* (pp. 3–12). Sage.

Epstein, S. (1973). The self-concept revisited: Or a theory of a theory. *American Psychologist*, *28*(5), 404–416. doi:10.1037/h0034679

Erikson, E. H. (1968). *Identity: Youth and crisis*. Norton.

Fearon, J. D. (1999). *What is identity (as we now use the word)?* [Unpublished manuscript]. Stanford University. https://web.stanford.edu/group/fearon-research/cgi-bin/wordpress/wp-content/uploads/2013/10/What-is-Identity-as-we-now-use-the-word-.pdf

Land, R. (2014, July). *Liminality close-up* [Paper presentation]. HECU7 at Lancaster University.

Leavy, P. (2015). *Method meets art: Arts-based research practice* (2nd ed.). Guilford Press.

Marcia, J. E. (1966). Development and validation of ego-identity status. *Journal of Personality and Social Psychology, 3*(5), 551–558. https://doi.org/10.1037/h0023281

Meyer, J. H. F., & Land, R. (2005). Threshold concepts and troublesome knowledge (2): Epistemological considerations and a conceptual framework for teaching and learning. *Higher Education, 49*(3), 373–388. https://doi.org/10.1007/s10734-004-6779-5

Meyer, J. H. F., & Land, R. (Eds.). (2006). *Overcoming barriers to student understanding: Threshold concepts and troublesome knowledge.* Routledge.

Piaget, J. (1976). Piaget's theory. In B. Inhelder & C. Zwingmann (Eds.), *Piaget and his school: A reader in developmental psychology* (pp. 11–23). Springer.

Rattray, J. (2016). Affective dimensions of liminality. In R. Land, J. H. F. Meyer, & M. T. Flanagan (Eds.), *Threshold concepts in practice* (pp. 67–76). Sense.

Van Hoof, A. (1997). *Identity formation in adolescence: Structural integration and guiding influences* [Unpublished PhD thesis]. Utrecht University.

Waterman, A. S. (1999). Identity, the identity statuses, and identity status development: A contemporary statement. *Developmental Review, 19*(4), 591–621. https://doi.org/10.1006/drev.1999.0493

CHAPTER 8

Discussion and Conclusion

1 Introduction

This book addresses the research question: To what extent can engagement in the visual art-making process foster the navigation of the liminal space? The basis for this research question originated in observations of my students who were engaging with troublesome life experiences through the art-making process. This was indicative of transformation or ontological shifts. Therefore, I pondered a fundamental question: What role does art making have in transformations that are evidenced in the art-making process? The implications of this research are intended to foster whole reflection upon pedagogy and learning environments, which may account for the epistemic element of visual art and the threshold concepts theoretical framework. As a result of contextualized reflection, the role of art education may become more than mere ornament (Eisner, 2008) and realize the essential element in education that it can be, especially in this time of important movement toward equity and cultural responsiveness.

The arts are often credited with developing critical thinking skills without acknowledging nuance or distinctions; therefore, I argue it is oversimplified to credit any "art making" as developing critical thinking. It is a potential outcome when the pedagogy and learning environment foster learning experiences that employ epistemic elements of the art-making process. The threshold concepts framework provides a lens that can bring such issues into focus through reflection upon pedagogy and learning environments as well as the nature of learning in visual art. Therefore, I became interested and curious in understanding this critical observation more deeply and pursued my research into threshold concepts and arrived at the significance of the liminal state as a necessary element to fostering critical thinking and human development.

This book intends to promote reflection regarding larger implications that can be acknowledged about the domain of art education in the twenty-first century. This book demonstrates several issues on this point. The case studies demonstrate unique and inherent qualities of visual art that are effectively understood through the semiotic lens. Especially when the liminal space clearly involves profoundly affective elements, the ability to form or express linguistic signs is quite difficult if not impossible. The art-making process was clearly discussed by all, of the young people, as providing an ability to engage with troublesome knowledge and liminality without the reliance upon the

© KONINKLIJKE BRILL NV, LEIDEN, 2022 | DOI:10.1163/9789004508132_008

formation of linguistic signs. The dialogic element extends beyond the use of visual signs for self-expression and communication with others; more importantly, for introspective reflection to engage experiences and make meaning from them. In short, the arts can act as a unique vehicle to traverse the liminal space and provide a unique means to glimpse subjective experience of the liminal state. The visual arts can provide a visual record of the felt experience of individuals as they cross thresholds and traverse the liminal space with a context provided when linguistic signs are able to be formed and articulated in the act of personal reflection.

2 Visual Art and the Complex Threshold Concept of Self and Voice

Meaning making, therefore, is not an abstract idea. Meaning making is impossible outside of the individual and therefore the knowledge gained is "embodied" knowledge. It is for this reason that Mezirow (1991) suggests that the self-image of the learner should be considered as part of the learning context (Blackie et al., 2010, p. 4).

The opening quote is succinct in explicating issues relevant to self as a complex or thorny threshold. Land (2014, p. 2) places emphasis upon the role of transformation in threshold concepts as being "superordinate and non-negotiable" and making meaning of our experiences is an underpinning assumption of transformative theory (Mezirow, 2000). However, transformations or ontological shifts occur within the self and involve the self. Moreover, liminal journeys, for these young people, involve affective elements connected to their own troublesome life experience. This affective involvement has proven to complicate and even impede the progression of these young people.

The case studies of these art students focused on their sense of self being interrupted due to their respective experienced troublesomeness. In this case the self is understood as an internal experience of intimate feelings that are integral to the subjective understanding of self (Cooley, 2011). This represents troublesome knowledge as well as the vessel in which the liminal state is experienced and the threshold in which a reidentity occurs. "In a preliminary stage, a learner's tacit views are interrupted as she is introduced to and begins to grapple with a threshold concept" (Adler-Kassner et al., 2012, p. 2).

The art-making process always involves the self and this is true in these case studies. In the cases of Jayden, Aline, and Rene, the making of meaning is a highly personal manner of "opening up a new and previously inaccessible way of thinking about something" (Land et al., 2005, p. 53). However, the vehicle through which these new understandings are reached is the art-making process, and the vessel in which this navigation occurs is the self. The newly

DISCUSSION AND CONCLUSION

articulated understandings reside in the artwork and involve the epistemic, expressive, and dialogic elements of their artwork. Within the self the understandings originate in the cognitive and affective dimension of experience, but are given form through semiotic aspects of art making. All four of the young people reflected upon their inability to employ linguistic signs and the involvement of affect as powerful and consistently present; without a transformed understanding of self, the young people could not progress (Land et al., 2005). In fact, the young people described self-destructive behavior and feelings of self-hatred, anger, and fear.

These young people demonstrate profound courage and strength in their ability to persevere and ultimately progress toward transformation after prolonged states of being stuck. Moreover, the ability of the young people to employ art as a means of navigating the liminal space or tunnel highlights complexity of self as a threshold. They had to engage the art-making process with enough depth and sincerity that the tacit was given form, despite the power and presence of the affective dimension. The young people had to be willing to interpret and reflect upon the expressed content of their work, possibly generating feelings of being vulnerable and reviving the troublesome knowledge with its affective elements.

As an educator, I feel this highlights the importance of the threshold lens and semiotic pedagogy as these liminal experiences are psychological and emotional. Therefore, the ability to understand and facilitate cannot be offered through lecture or in a role of gatekeeper. I must empower the individual to reflect on the self and assist in interpreting and creating meaning. As an educator, I am not trying to develop artists; I am trying to develop human beings and challenge them to engage with troublesome feelings and experiences. I hope to foster the ability of each young person to understand media and material as a vehicle to represent their psychological and emotional selves.

The idea of art as meaning making can be articulated as "voice." Jayden, Aline, Rene, and Cade reflect upon the importance that "voice" provided in their liminal journey toward healing the self. In documenting their liminal transformations and reidentity, I find that art as "voice" is not only a way to gain insight into liminal experiences but has become a kind of threshold. "Threshold concepts are defined as concepts that bind a subject together, being fundamental to ways of thinking and practicing in that discipline" (Land et al., 2005, p. 54). It was understanding this that helped them unlock other things or make other transformations.

> [A]s students acquire threshold concepts, and extend their use of language in relation to these concepts, there occurs also a shift in the learner's subjectivity, a repositioning of the self. [...] What is being emphasized

here is the inter-relatedness of the learner's identity with thinking and language. Threshold concepts lead not only to transformed thought but to a transfiguration of identity and adoption of an extended discourse. (Meyer & Land 2005, cited in Land et al., 2005, p. 58)

This statement by Meyer and Land assumes the use of language as being linguistic signs. The cases presented in this book clearly demonstrate that art is a visual language that is comprised of personal visual signs that are injected with emotion and experience. Jayden, Aline, Rene, and Cade all extended their use of language in the only manner or media they were capable of utilizing. As a result, their identity or self evolved with the clarity of their visual language. These four young people all stated that visual art did not solve their issues or fix anything. But they did say that visual art was the only manner in which they could engage with, or wrap their heads around, their troublesome knowledge. The difficulties and anguish were always present, but until they experienced the potential of the art-making process, they had no means to understand their thoughts and feelings. The art-making process was a means to give voice to the self in their liminal state and evolve to ontological shifts.

3   **Visual Art Navigating the Affective Dimension and the Stuck Place**

This section will discuss the impact of the affective dimension upon Jayden, Aline, Rene, and Cade as well as its relationship to the liminal experience and the navigation of the liminal space. Walker (2013) describes the impact of affective elements of the liminal state, which is clearly relevant to these case studies. For example, Walker (2013) describes the power of the affective element being capable to hold an individual in a stuck place (Ellsworth, 1989, 1997; Meyer & Land, 2005).

Here they will experience the strong affective component of [threshold concepts]. There will be "cognitive dissonance," a motivational drive to reduce unpleasant feelings of uncertainty, and "perseverance," in which more familiar courses of action will continue to be employed despite evidence to the contrary. Too much uncertainty in this liminal state and the learner will not be able to progress beyond a surface understanding. (Walker, 2013, p. 250)

These young people were overwhelmed by the affective element of the liminal state and were incapable of progressing until they found a means of

DISCUSSION AND CONCLUSION

engagement that provided an ability to process the emotions that were inextricable from troublesome experience. Jayden, Aline, Rene, and Cade experienced an interruption of the self (Adler-Kassner et al., 2012) which impacted the cognitive abilities for linguistic knowledge and signs.

Stuck places can be conceptualized as epistemological obstacles "that block any transformed perspective" (Brousseau, 1997, cited in Meyer & Land, 2005, p. 377). The stated remedy for these epistemological obstacles is constructive feedback that gets to the source and overcomes such barriers (Meyer & Land, 2005). However, the idea of constructive feedback is oversimplified or understated in the full context of learning environments, especially in the context of the art-learning environment. Biggs (1999) and Ellsworth (1989, 1997) argues for the necessity of pedagogy and learning environments that embrace the uncertainty and complexity of the affective and social aspects of student subjectivity. The observations of this research inform my argument as to the importance of semiotic pedagogy and the inherent dialogic of the visual art-making process as a means of facilitating the navigation of the affective component of stuck places. In other words, semiotic pedagogy informs us to embrace the student's past experiences and resulting perspective in order to build upon them. In my experience, this can be empowering for students and allow for more honest dialogue between educators and students. Moreover, the semiotic and dialogic aspects of the art-making process can also act as a form feedback either with the self or from an educator through interpretation of visual signs and symbols.

Cousin (2003) argues there is an ontological dimension in stuck places which puts emphasis upon the reality of the internal experience of a stuck place, particularly as it pertains to the affective element. A pedagogy that attempts through instruction a means to navigate these feelings is assuming there is potential for an understanding (by the individual) of the complexity of the affective experience in the liminal state. There is an interrelationship of the affective and cognitive dimensions that impacts the formation of language and presumably clarity of thought. The inherent advantage of the art-making process is the construction of knowledge that can simultaneously involve the affective and the cognitive dimensions. As I documented the young people's liminal journey through their portfolios, there is a clarity of visual language that is progressive and suggests the increased involvement of the cognitive dimension.

The learning environment that I attempt to foster embraces the semiotic element of art making and allows me to be sensitive to meanings that may be tacit for the students. This was certainly the case for Jayden, Aline, and Cade, while Rene intentionally engaged me through visual signs. The point is that constructive feedback can involve sensitivity to the affective and cognitive dimensions by focusing upon the artwork as an expression of knowledge. If emphasis is placed entirely upon formal visual elements, then I am ignoring the essential motivations for creating the artwork. The constructive feedback primarily comes in the form of questions about the artwork to which the student responds and is a private discussion. This process allows the student to have a visual sign to put context, form, or meaning to their underpinning intentions. Quite often this leads to more personal discussions and clarity of intent in both the work and the individual. Jayden, Aline, Rene, and Cade were able to put words and cognitive understanding to their liminal journey because it is less threatening to talk about or through their artwork. The work can convey the power of nonlinguistic knowledge and feeling (Langer, 1957).

At points the young people were able to progress further into their liminal tunnel and this seems to coincide with changes in the sophistication and clarity of their visual language. "In a liminal stage, the learner begins to enact that knowledge; at the same time, she becomes aware of her work with the concept and her interactions with it" (Adler-Kassner et al., 2012, p. 2). The more substantive work suggests the young people developing awareness and employing visual art as a vehicle for navigating the liminal space.

Land, Rattray, and Vivian (2014, p. 6) discuss the necessity that "learners need to engage with and manipulate conceptual materials, that is, the physical means of describing, discussing and exploring concepts." I argue this book is an extension of this claim with more profound circumstances.

4 Visual Art as Semiotic Dialogue

There is a unique interrelationship between linguistic and nonlinguistic language. The students do not have the words to convey and process their respective troublesome ontological states but the art-making process can facilitate a means to understand these associated feelings and understand aspects of self. The semiotic aspect of the art-making process provides an opportunity for internal dialogue that is safe and private. This section will focus upon the element of semiotic dialogue as it relates to the young people and threshold crossing.

"As learners move through these liminal stages, their knowledge also becomes less tacit and more explicit, discursive, and conscious, at least for a time – they not only know what they know, but they are also more likely to recognize how they know it" (Adler-Kassner et al., 2012, p. 2). Jayden, Aline, Rene, and Cade all highlight a dialogic component of the art-making process which involves an expressive element as well as the introspective element of this dialogic process. In the cases of Rene and Aline, I argue each can give voice to hidden pain and the ability to hold conversations with the self were of equal importance in navigating the liminal space. This is particularly relevant to the healing aspect of accepting their past experiences as well as ontological shifts. In the cases of Jayden and Cade, the dialogic element is most relevant to a dialogue with the self. Jayden describes herself as split and embracing different attributes as social situations dictated, which involved many racist interactions that perpetuated troublesomeness with her concept of self. I believe the art-making process and meeting her birth father facilitated the processing of feelings about self.

Cade is similar to Jayden in the sense that understanding identity and self was troublesome. Cade did not describe himself as split or having versions of himself, but he did try to deny or keep a true version of himself from evolving. The art-making process, acceptance from friends, and finding love arguably facilitated his journey through the liminal space and empower his ability to accept the self and align with identity.

In the case of Rene, she intentionally exploited the semiotic element of visual signs with the initial intention of provoking me with her silhouette piece. Rene used art in order to give voice to the troubling affective elements of her experience but also as a means of engaging with me as a participant in her liminal journey. As her portfolio evolved, the visual signs that Rene chose to employ focused on inviting others into a semiotic discourse. For example, the use of literal doors and her cast hand and the public mural were all attempts on her part to involve others with her internal dialogue; but there is a safety in the semiotic discourse of visual signs. There is a vulnerability without the embarrassment of confessing intimate details.

Aline's semiotic dialogue is extreme and powerful. In her case she involved a performative element which was a form or reliving horrible experiences or reengaging troubling mind spaces. In the making of her piece *Institution*, Aline literally reread excerpts from a journal about her most painful experiences. While her piece uses linguistic signs, the power and meaning of her voice lies in the more visual or performative aspects of the work. The words fall short of expressing what the marks and application of the material convey. The clawing and smacking of the walls with ink in combination with the language begins to express her internal experiences. More importantly, the performative element of the work is astonishingly brave and indicative of commitment to voice. The mere act of going through this psychological and emotional action is quite moving. Aline stated that she revealed past experiences in the making of this piece that she had never been able to convey. The public display and warm reception by visitors to the exhibition was a healing experience for Aline, which is like the experience of Rene and her public work. Aline was fearful of how others may judge or perceive her work and she did not expect such a positive and empathic response. Therefore, the actual doing or making, the public presentation, and the viewer response were all elements of the dialogic for Aline.

Jayden evolved her visual language from loose references to African culture into explicit commentary on racism and racial identity in the United States. This developed sophistication required a cognitive element and a clarity of intention. Her final video piece *Transformation* uses simple references to skin color. However, the action of the application and removal of the paint provides visual signs of her affective struggle in the liminal journey. Jayden refers to the piece as a reliving of a long transformative experience in the acceptance of self.

Cade uses symbols that make literal reference to voice, which was intentional once the mouths began to appear in his work. Previously, his work focused more upon mood and emotional states with which he struggled as a part of his journey to accepting himself as a gay man. The subtle changes in how he portrayed mouths document a clarity and empowerment for him to be open and accept the self.

The visual arts served as a vehicle for navigation of the liminal space through its inherent semiotic and dialogic elements. Even though, the young people do not credit the art making with moving beyond their troublesome state or the crossing of thresholds, they do credit art making with providing a means to engage with troublesome knowledge and involve the cognitive dimension more completely and with depth. This semiotic dialogue was internal and a form of voice that was expressed visually and engaged others with the nature of their lived experience. This dialogic reveals the affective experience but does not rely on the use of linguistic signs, which had proven to be difficult or frustrating. The affective dimension of troublesome knowledge and the liminal state was a part of their waking and tacit knowledge; visual art making provided an opportunity to engage with these feelings and give them form and shape, a more tangible entity. As something is given form it can be named and understood, allowing for a cognitive element to transition to awareness and understanding.

5 Pedagogy Informed by Semiotic Theory

> No thought exists without a sustaining support. (Mel Bochner)

The case studies in this book document the liminal journey of Jayden, Aline, Rene, and Cade with the intention of addressing implications for the classroom

DISCUSSION AND CONCLUSION

environment. The quote by Mel Bochner highlights the importance of art educators to reflect upon the relevance of the epistemic elements of the art-making process. I argue that art educators must understand art through the lens of semiotics in order to assist students in their use of art for making meaning and movement through the liminal space. Art educators can arrive at a means to access the more intrapersonal aspects of the student's art-making process by asking pointed and relevant questions informed by semiotic awareness.

This section will discuss the relevance of selected constructs of pedagogical content knowledge (PCK) and discuss their association to the liminal experience and the role of art making in the case studies presented. I will also clarify some of the PCK constructs where I believe it is relevant to better describe the experience of the young people from the pedagogical perspective.

The threshold literature introduces pedagogical content-knowledge (Shulman, 1987; Land et al., 2014), which provides pedagogical constructs that are informed by semiotics and discussed in this section. According to Land, Rattray, and Vivian (2014, p.205), "[a] teacher draws on PCK when putting him- or herself in the position of the learner." Shulman (1987, p. 4) states that PCK demonstrates an understanding on the part of the educator as to how "particular topics, problems or issues are organized, represented, and adapted to the diverse interests and abilities of learners, and presented for instruction."

Land et al. (2005) identify nine implications of threshold concepts for curriculum implementation, several of which hold relevance for this book: engagement, listening for understanding, reconstitution of self, and tolerating uncertainty.

Engagement is described as the need for students to manipulate conceptual materials which often involves graphic representation or communication (Land et al., 2014). Engagement directly involves the affective dimension which arguably is a launching pad for the visual representation and manipulation of conceptual materials. In the case of Jayden, Aline, Rene, and Cade, the manipulation of conceptual materials is a form of reflection and making meaning through the art-making process. It is important to highlight that the meaning of the artwork was at first tacit and the decision to make art about their previous experiences was not a conscious one. As the year progressed and I probed for the intention or meaning of the artwork with each student, clarity evolved. More specifically, as the young people analyzed the meaning of their artwork, they began to understand and perceive the relationship of the artworks to their past experiences and their feelings about those experiences. Moreover, as the students obtained this clarity the artwork became increasingly potent and deliberate.

Listening for understanding is another relevant implication of threshold concepts theory. Land, Rattray, and Vivian (2014) state that crossing thresholds will result in a new dialect, but signifiers can remain the same, therefore the new understandings may not be evident. In other words, the knowledge may have evolved but the individual will still rely upon existing signs to convey meaning, which can be flawed (Land et al., 2014). There must be new signifiers to match new knowledge or understandings. However, the art-making process is personal and an expressive visual language involving a form of signs and symbols that arguably fosters the individual's ability to arrive at a point of clarity and communication. More specifically, threshold concepts have a cognitive element, but they can be affective in nature and visual art provides the young people with the ability to arrive at the cognitive element by navigating the affective. Therefore, listening for understanding is also meant as interpreting images and discussing their potential meaning with students. In many cases, the visual representations may exceed the limitations of words in their understanding of experiences. However, as the student moves through the liminal space and crosses thresholds, the linguistic aspect of the understanding becomes more prevalent.

Reconstitution of self is another construct identified in PCK which is discussed in this section. While the essence of the construct is applicable to my arguments, there are some differences that I need to clarify that make them more interrelated to this book and the case studies presented. Land, Rattray, and Vivian (2014) describe reconstitution of self as resulting from the acquisition of a concept. Meyer and Land (2003, p. 9) identify multiple characteristics of threshold concepts; one being integrative in that "it exposes the previously hidden interrelatedness of something." The relevance of this is that as Land, Rattray, and Vivian (2014) argue that the acquisition of a concept can possess an integrative effect and change the perception by the individual toward many concepts and, ultimately, affect their worldview. However, it is important to highlight the distinction between the discussion in the literature and this book. The literature suggests that a reconstitution of self is a possible outcome of the liminal journey. However, the reconstitution of self is the core of the liminal journey and threshold crossing for Jayden, Aline, Rene, and Cade. I find it important to explicate this issue because the young people engage with much more powerful emotions than uncertainty or conceptual difficulty. Moreover, due to the role of the art-making process, the issue of boundedness becomes more relevant than integrative in the context of this book. The art-making process acts as a "bridging function" which "refers to ongoing, two-sided actions and interactions between contexts" (Akkerman & Bakker, 2011, p. 136). As previously stated, the art-making process acts as an epistemic vehicle that provides a unique ability to navigate the liminal space and therefore the issue of boundary crossing is more relevant to a reconstitution of self than previously hidden conceptual relatedness of concepts.

DISCUSSION AND CONCLUSION

Tolerating uncertainty is the next construct of PCK whose relevance to this book will be discussed. Tolerating uncertainty is a relevant construct but is also understated in Land, Rattray, and Vivian (2014), as it pertains to this book and the experience of Jayden, Aline, Rene, and Cade. The discussion shall describe the construct and explicate its importance to the young people's liminal experience.

Land, Rattray, and Vivian (2014) describe tolerating uncertainty with the assumptions of academic learning and the vacillation between certainty and uncertainty concerning new concepts. The reflective process informs the student's ability to move beyond the acceptance of teacher suggestions at face value and exercise judgment that requires prolonged inquiry (Land et al., 2014; Dewey, 1997). While reflection is certainly an element of the semiotic aspect of this book, the young people have struggled for many years with powerful feelings and experiences that have impact upon their sense of self. Therefore, the construct of vital experience (Dewey, 1916) is also on point. More specifically, Dewey (1916) argues that the role of education is to foster the desire in young people to engage with troublesome knowledge. Jayden, Aline, Rene, and Cade moved beyond reflection upon concepts and used art to engage with troublesome knowledge, making the art education experience one of relevance and vital experience.

There is some literature specific to the domain of art education that addresses semiotic pedagogy. Specifically, Smith-Shank (1995) introduces the construct of collateral experience, which also holds relevance for the art-making process in the case studies presented.

The argument being raised is that the construction of knowledge and understanding is subjective and that conventions of school subjects can be artificial and overly constraining when rigidly adhered to. Smith-Shank (1995) argues that the diminished value of art education, in the curriculum of schools, is due to its comfort to remain within its own artificial boundaries and any enhanced relevance in education relies on the ability of art educators to remove the constraints. I believe this removal of artificial constraints in art education can be informed by semiotic pedagogy.

The construct of collateral experience is integral to the arguments I am making about the relationship between art education and semiotic theory. Collateral experience is "previous experience which makes a novel situation accessible" (Smith-Shank, 1995, p. 235) and is the deliberate empowerment of students to employ their own life experience as context in the classroom. In my view, this also holds associations with issues of equity and cultural responsiveness discussed in Chapter 2. This construct also holds similarities to schema (Piaget, 1976) and the recognized importance of prior knowledge in constructivist views of learning. However, an important distinction is that prior knowledge in the education context can imply a domain-specific association with the learning of new concepts. According to Smith-Shank (1995), collateral experience in the semiotic framework implies that a vast array of experiences can be of value in the construction of knowledge and expression of meaning or understanding. The implication being that historically determined disciplinary boundaries can constrain learning: "[W]hen learning is understood as thinking, it is a process and not a product. It becomes an ongoing process of inquiry which cannot be defined by the limits of subject matter" (Smith-Shank, 1995, p. 236).

The discussion as to the relevance of semiotics intends to substantiate observations within this book to relevant literature, as they pertain to pedagogy and learning in the art environment. In the context of art education, the opening quotation from Mel Bochner highlights a need for consideration of the cognitive and affective dimensions of learning and particularly within the threshold concepts framework. The affective complexity becomes an element in understanding the liminal space (Land, et al., 2014; Rattray, 2016); and pedagogy that is sensitive to the liminal experience must involve elements of subjective experiences within the learning environment. Smith-Shank (1995) argues the need for the subject of art to expand beyond its conceptual boundaries and exploit its inherent constructivist and semiotic nature for more compelling and authentic learning. I argue that pedagogy informed by semiotics can embrace individual students and their unique prior experiences in a manner that allows the art-making process to make meaning out of existing and new knowledge.

An important implication of PCK and art-learning environments that are informed by semiotic theory is the building of relationships with students. The case studies presented and the discussion on semiotic pedagogy suggest the likelihood of students creating highly personal and expressive artwork. I argue the issue of positionality becomes important when an art-learning environment fosters a semiotic approach to the art-making process.

6   Engaging with Liminality and Psychological Safety

The case studies in this book involve young people who engage with profoundly troubling experiences and in two of the cases these experiences without question involve trauma. In Chapter 1, I provide an ethical framework for how I proceeded to work with these students and I also use these same guidelines for all students whether I am writing about the individual or not. The ethical framework is based on proper notification to adults and school counselors to ensure the safety of students. This topic requires more discussion as I am writing this book to argue the merits of engaging with liminality and troublesome knowledge that involves difficulty, risk, and powerful elements of transformation. The risk is primarily the students' willingness to engage with relevant life experience and for me as an educator in the facilitating of this learning. The ethical guidelines I have in place are my best effort to allow the opportunity for this work to be done in the context of a classroom with safety nets in place in case someone is overwhelmed.

However, I think two important elements of this are found in the necessity of establishing relationships and the reality that Jayden, Aline, Rene, and Cade were all the driving forces behind the artwork that was being made. In other words, as a result of feeling psychological and emotional safety the students felt they could engage with more personal and profound experiences in their artwork. As I have previously stated, there is no specific assignment designed to direct students to express such experiences, nor would I view such an approach valuable. I argue the nature of the learning environment and the relationships formed empowered students to understand art making as an opportunity.

Rogers (1983), Barnett (2007) and Blackie, Case, and Jawitz (2010) discuss student centeredness as the involvement of "being" and "self," with an emphasis upon the genuine relationships formed between teacher and student. The teacher should always be represented by their genuine self with concern about the development of the being of the individual. This is particularly relevant in the art-learning environment; I consider the student/teacher relationship as rich fertilizer for personal engagement with the art-making process that addresses relevant experience and genuine visual expression. The nature of genuine results is not based on the formal qualities of the artwork but on the visual signs or visual language of the young person and the conviction and substantive use of visual language for authentic expressive purpose. In my experience, as students develop genuine work, they are more apt to understand how to develop their visual language into more compelling and sophisticated expression.

Emotional and psychological safety are essential within the daily activity of the art-learning environment (Catherall, 2006); more specifically, it needs to be an environment that fosters security in being vulnerable and authentic. In my view, it is part of the role of the art educator to challenge students to experiment and extend their visual work into new arenas which may involve troublesome experiences and, potentially, trauma. When one considers ideas related to trauma-informed classrooms, the work I have done with Jayden, Aline, Rene, and Cade may seem problematic. Trauma-informed classrooms consider the impact of trauma and value the recognition of the signs and symptoms of trauma within individuals in order to actively resist retraumatization (SAMHSA, 2016; Pickens & Tschopp, 2017). As I stated earlier in this section and different aspects of the case studies, the students have all chosen to employ their art-making process to engage their respective experiences. My selection of them as case studies came as a result of recognizing important elements in their work and responding accordingly. The trauma-informed practices outlined in Pickens and Tschopp (2017) emphasize the acknowledgement of previous experience and fostering respectful relationships as a result. The approaches toward my ethical obligations were to ensure I do not attempt to engage in a form of therapy but rather alert those around me so proper discussions and safety nets can be in place. My emphasis – and I believe the emphasis of any art educator – is to be cognizant of the line between art therapy and the therapeutic value of making art.

The nature of challenging the students and facilitating profound engagement does not occur through confrontation or a stated list of expectations. Instead, the issue is empowerment through relationships founded on trust and respect. I do not require students to make artwork about emotionally complex experiences. The nature of the assignments and the depth of discourse about the creative process can empower students to employ the art-making process in ways they find rewarding. There are many students who create powerful work that is not biographical or drenched with angst or pain, but learning environments that establish and permeate emotional safety provide the opportunity for students to explore and engage with these feelings.

I believe my experiences as a visual artist and a recovering alcoholic and drug addict are important personal attributes in my learning environment and in the relationships established with the students. It can be argued that my interest and understanding of the threshold concepts framework are directly related to these experiences. My extensive studio art background underpins my teaching of visual art as being inherently epistemic. In this sense, it expresses knowledge and acts as a form of knowledge construction. Therefore, the creative process and the struggle to conceptualize and express one's ideas or feelings are the most important aspects of education in the arts. As a result, I can perceive and understand intentions in the artwork from the student's perspective. My interpretation of student work is informed within a semiotic context and not only an aesthetic and skill-based lens. More specifically, the ability to understand the semiotics of visual language informs my ability to ask questions that can slowly uncover deeper and complex meaning that may be held tacit by the student. Therefore, the arrival at clarity is established through discourse and observation as opposed to a pointed discussion.

My struggles with drugs and alcohol (which resulted in sobriety) is something that is well known in my classroom. In general, this reality has been a source of help (although often futile) for students, parents, and other teachers during my years as an educator. However, I learned in the course of this study that the struggles I experienced became a source of credibility and relationship building with Jayden, Aline, Rene, and Cade. In different moments each of the young people had brought up my willingness to share my struggles with them as being important. The implication from the different conversations (some of which occurred after the students graduated) was that I had already engaged a form of troublesome knowledge and transformed as a result. This allowed them to feel empowered to do the same and that the complex experiences could be understood or navigated. The next section will evolve the discussion by focusing upon issues associated with curriculum and learning.

7   Implications for Curriculum and Learning in the Visual Art Classroom

This section focuses upon issues of curriculum and learning in the context of visual art-learning environments as is relevant to this book. In the previous section I argued that the role of pedagogy and the art educator is to facilitate engagement with the liminal experience and supporting young people in its navigation. It is important to keep in mind that not all students have trauma in their past and the profundity of the liminal experience will vary in complexity and content. The case studies in this book were chosen because they demonstrate an engagement with art making that results in transformation associated with profound life experience. Obviously, not all students have such experiences in their past but there is a need for all learners no matter how typical to experience such powerful learning through the art-making process.

Contextualized within this research, Elgin (2010) discusses the important distinctions between imitation and understanding that can be considered in the context of art education. Quite literally, art education can often be limited to a means of imitation or is mimetic (Elgin, 2010). Imitation in secondary art education (in my experience) is more accurately conceptualized as a perpetuation of art primarily as a demonstration of skill and pleasing aesthetics, reducing the learning tasks to sets of unusual instructions to be followed. However, the art-making process is a means of understanding as evidenced in the cases presented of Jayden, Aline, Rene, and Cade. As previously discussed, these young people experienced ontological shifts and resubjectivity through the semiotic dialogue of visual art making. This dialogue has allowed these young people a means to engage with troublesome experience that had remained with them for many years and to reformulate identity and self that encompasses these experiences and not merely dictated by them.

The issue of the gatekeeper and the curriculum as a living entity (Irwin & Chalmers, 2007) becomes highly relevant in this discussion. The opportunity to engage relevant life experiences with art making would not present itself if I dictated the terms of artistic engagement. The distinction being made is summarized in the following quote: "Curriculum-as-plan is often concerned with a subject-based approach and attends to experiencing the visual. Curriculum-as-lived is often concerned with a student- or society-based perspective, and attends to visualizing experiences" (Irwin & Chalmers, 2007, p. 179).

Pedagogy and curriculum that facilitate engagement with the liminal experience manifest as an empowering of students to express themselves with bravery and without preconception. In this expressive process one begins to perceive a self that may be less familiar but all too present. The semiotic pedagogy and embracing the dialogic nature of visual signs is crucial in this context of challenging students to experience expression and voice as a threshold. In the case of Jayden, Aline, Rene, and Cade, my facilitation of their learning, in large part, occurs through a semiotic discourse. In other words, my ability to perceive, interpret, and inquire about their visual signs slowly unpacked meaning and its interrelationship with life experiences and tacit knowledge.

Irwin and Chalmers (2007, pp. 179–180) further explain: "Both interpretations of art education curricula involve a visual component and an experiential component, though one interpretation understands curriculum (and art) primarily as a noun (plan), while the other understands curriculum (and art) primarily as a verb (lived)." This articulates an essential issue in the consideration of art-learning environments through the threshold concepts framework. As an education process, art is often misconstrued as an end point that students need to prove themselves worthy or deserving by following along a teacher-prescribed path. In my experience, art is a mechanism or vehicle for the navigation of complex thoughts, feelings, and experiences. By giving form and representation to lived experiences and feelings, individuals engage in the making of meaning that may only be accessible through a visual art-making process.

8 Assessment of Learning in the Art Environment

The previous discussion informed by Irwin and Chalmers (2007) focuses on lived experience of the curriculum, which holds roots in Dewey (1916) and vital experience. While such literature is important and insightful, it does not

DISCUSSION AND CONCLUSION

address the practical challenges facing art educators: specifically, the current assessment-driven climate of education and the culture of mastery, results, and quantified data. When one considers the artwork produced by Jayden, Aline, Rene, and Cade, it is impressive in some regards, but its power is realized in the context of the student and their experiences. The students did fine in their high-stakes assessment, but they did not get top marks as their learning may indicate they should have. Although not a true concern for this book (nor myself), it does raise questions. The work is a mature and sophisticated journey through complex aspects of the liminal space. Do we place prescribed visual standards on students regarding assessment? Where is the true value of the art experience? It is the visual result or the conveying of complex experience? This issue is increasingly frustrating as many current assessment practices place value upon concrete rubrics and scoring. However, as this book indicates, the value of the art experience is messy and less concrete than what public education prefers. As discussed throughout this book, there are many learning environments that remain a form of mimicry and lack a substantive engagement with the art-making process. However, these types of learning environments may represent the types of tasks and indications of learning that any US schools desire. The next section evolves this issue in addressing implications for policy.

9 Implications for Education Policy and Learning Environments

In the course of conducting this research I have clarified and arrived at a deeper understanding of pedagogy and learning in the visual art environment. As a result, I hope and believe that I have become a more effective educator to my students, in a broader sense. Obviously, this book was written simultaneous to my continued employment in the public-school sector. In this process I have continuously encountered experiences that have become increasingly troubling and a likely consequence for educators that work with students in a personal and intensive manner. In my area of the United States there is a great deal of discussion on the necessity of building relationships with students as a means of fostering intrinsic motivation (Ryan & Deci, 2000). There is also a lot of emphasis in my area upon equity and culturally responsive teaching and I truly believe these policy efforts are positive and necessary. I also believe that building relationships is at the core of establishing equity and culturally responsive environments in the visual art-learning environment and the result of building meaningful relationships can be more complex than we may expect.

An element of this book, as discussed earlier, is the importance of establishing relationships and trust with students so the learning environment becomes a space of emotional safety for students. I believe I am successful (as many teachers are) at creating this type of space and, as a result, students begin to express feelings, thoughts, and experiences that matter to them. As the case studies present, this is not necessarily a conscious decision and obviously there is no manner of task to be assigned that directly results in the types of artwork presented in this book. In other words, I do not assign students to make work about their most painful experiences in life. Instead, the semiotic element of visual art can act as a vehicle for nonlinguistic navigation of liminal space and tacit knowledge can be given form and ultimately linguistic signs. These more personal and profound experiences are arguably even more likely to be expressed when we are successful in building trust with students and environments that are permeated with emotional and psychological safety.

A problem arises in the hypocrisy of differing entities involved in or surrounding the educational systems and its oversimplified use of the word "(in)appropriate." More specifically, I have had quality student artwork removed from exhibition or needed to defend a student's use of images or words. While this book demonstrates (and my personal views fully support) a code of ethics that prioritizes the safety of students, above all else, these types of interventions most often have nothing to do with student safety. Instead, they are about protecting a school system or not wanting to deal with the reality faced by some of the young people in the school. When I present in educational conferences, I often encounter art teachers who get angry at the rawness of the student work I present, or I get asked why I let students make this kind of work. In a summer program that I frequently teach, parents and teachers have complained at the disturbing nature of some of the work the students create and, in some cases, administrators have removed work from the walls. While my main school is not usually like this, the climate is such that it is a possibility. But, in my experience, students are not usually upset or disrupted by such work; it is the adults who have issues with the work and the schools are somehow compelled to keep these darker realities from being seen. In my experience, when we truly connect with students the artwork they make can challenge those around them and it is not always met with celebration and interest; rather, the works can evoke outrage, fear, and difficulty.

The previous context is meant to raise an argument regarding school policy and the need for nuance because complexity in the classrooms are often only judged in terms of black and white and not with any context. Therefore, I have proposed, with no success, that there be an adoption of additional policy that

DISCUSSION AND CONCLUSION 151

targets the arts specifically. Currently, most administrators only have a standardized set of rules that address behavior, appropriate dress, drugs and alcohol, violence, and other related topics. These are necessary but they are blanket policies that disregard the act of self-expression in a creative environment designed to foster such activity. This is the primary problem in the summer program. Administrators or parents are not always used to visual arts that go beyond aesthetic exercises and nice design. Therefore, it can be perceived as a threat and/ or danger of some sort. Obviously, the truth of the issue is that the vital experience (Dewey, 1916) for some students is quite troubling and its visual representation quite challenging. In fairness, these types of stress are not daily occurrences and there are many that understand and celebrate the value of these learning experiences. However, the negative elements do occur, and they are quite stressful; they often cause me to question my own judgment on a deeper level if it had not already been called into question by another individual.

As a response, I wish to highlight the need for school systems to adopt nuanced policies in their understanding of visual expression. For example, a drawing of a weapon is not a weapon nor a sign of a desire for violence. In fact, it could (and often is) an image used to make statements about peace. Nudity is not pornography or sexually explicit content. A painting of a body clawing at its face is not necessarily a literal desire to perform this action. There are many personal examples I can provide, but it would require lengthy explanation; therefore, I wish simply to get the point across. Even in the case of a supportive administration, when issue is taken with student artwork, principals only have generic sets of rules as guideline to formulate their response. Therefore, simple issues of reason can evolve into larger and more stressful experiences.

This book has intended to present visual art-learning environments and pedagogy through the lens of threshold concepts and semiotic theory. Consequently, I hope it provides an opportunity for reflection upon one's own approaches to the utilization of visual art in respective learning environments. Furthermore, I hope to present increased relevance and significance of the visual arts in education during the twenty-first century. In addition, I have realized that there are unique elements to art education that embrace vital experience, which requires an enhanced understanding and support from other facets of the school community. In my experience, these approaches have resulted in young people who engaged in authentic and relevant learning that has transformed and deepened an understanding of self. I argue that this book presents learning that is as important if not more important than any of their schooling for each of these young people and the others like them that were not a part of this book.

10 Consideration for Future Research and Recommendation for Art Education

This book makes the argument that to maintain or establish relevance as an important contributor to education we must turn to the epistemic potential of the art-making process. The construct of semiotic pedagogy establishes a series of concepts that can provide art educators with a means to understand the value and opportunity to establish deeper relationships with and understanding of students' experiences and tacit knowledge. The aim of this book is to provoke reflection in art educators upon their own pedagogy and understand obstacles that prevent students from engaging with relevant life experiences. As educators begin to understand the epistemic nature of the art-making process and the benefits of relationships established through semiotic pedagogy, our ability to involve liminality and troublesome knowledge will become increasingly clear and affective.

My future research will explore the potential of semiotic pedagogy as it integrates threshold concepts into the learning environment in ways that can benefit pedagogy in many different subject areas. This investigation inherently involves evolving understanding of the affective dimension in the art-learning environment and the benefits of semiotic pedagogy. Continual effort to understand the liminal experience is also an important direction for continued research. A focus upon case studies and the use of artwork can be a valuable means for continued in-depth study of the student learning experience and the way the art-making process can foster transformative learning. Furthermore, future case studies may involve students from a wider range of experiences that may or may not be as difficult as the case studies represented in this book. In addition, there is always interest in interdisciplinary uses of the visual arts as a means of traversing troublesome knowledge and the liminal space in different academic contexts.

References

Adler-Kassner, L., Majewski, J., & Koshnick, D. (2012). The value of troublesome knowledge: Transfer and threshold concepts in writing and history. *Composition Forum*, *26*. http://compositionforum.com/issue/26/troublesome-knowledge-threshold.php

Akkerman, S. F., & Bakker, A. (2011). Boundary crossing and boundary objects. *Review of Educational Research*, *81*(2), 132–169.

Barnett, R. (2007). *Will to learn: Being a student in an age of uncertainty*. McGraw-Hill Education.

DISCUSSION AND CONCLUSION

Biggs, J. B. (1999). *Teaching for quality learning at university*. Society for Research in Higher Education/Open University Press.

Blackie, M. A., Case, J. M., & Jawitz, J. (2010). Student-centredness: The link between transforming students and transforming ourselves. *Teaching in Higher Education*, *15*(6), 637–646.

Brousseau, G. (1997). *Theory of didactical situations in mathematics* (N. Balacheff, M. Cooper, R. Sutherland, & V. Warfield, Transl. and Ed.). Kluwer.

Catherall, D. R. (2006). *Emotional Safety: Viewing couples through the lens of affect*. Routledge.

Cooley, C. H. (2011). The looking-glass self. In Jodi O'Brien (Ed.), *The production of reality: Essays and readings on social interaction* (5th ed., pp. 126–128). Sage.

Cousin, G. (2003, August 26–30). *Threshold concepts, troublesome knowledge and learning about others* [Paper presentation]. The 10th conference of the European Association for Research on Learning and Instruction (EARLI), Padova, Italy.

Dewey, J. (1916). *Democracy and education: An introduction to the philosophy of education*. Macmillan.

Dewey, J. (1997). *How we think*. Courier Corporation.

Eisner, E. (2008). Art and knowledge. In J. G. Knowles & A. L. Cole (Eds.), *Handbook of the arts in qualitative research: Perspectives, methodologies, examples, and issues* (pp. 3–12). Sage.

Elgin, C. Z. (2010). Telling instances. In R. Frigg & M. Hunter (Eds.), *Beyond mimesis and convention: Representation in art and science* (pp. 1–17). Springer.

Ellsworth, E. (1989). Why doesn't this feel empowering? Working through the repressive myths of critical pedagogy. *Harvard Educational Review*, *59*(3), 297–325.

Ellsworth, E. (1997). *Teaching positions: Difference, pedagogy, and the power of address*. Teachers College Press.

Irwin, R. L., & Chalmers, F. G. (2007). Experiencing the visual and visualizing experiences. In L. Bresler (Ed.), *International handbook of research in arts education* (pp. 179–196). Springer.

Land, R. (2014, July). *Liminality close-up* [Paper presentation]. HECU7 at Lancaster University.

Land, R., Cousin, G., Meyer, J. H. F., & Davies, P. (2005). Threshold concepts and troublesome knowledge (3): Implications for course design and evaluation. In C. Rust (Ed.), *Improving student learning: Diversity and inclusivity* (pp. 53–64). Oxford Centre for Staff & Learning Development. https://www.ee.ucl.ac.uk/~mflanaga/ISL04-pp53-64-Land-et-al.pdf

Land, R., Rattray, J., & Vivian, P. (2014). Learning in the liminal space: A semiotic approach to threshold concepts. *Higher Education*, *67*(2), 199–217.

Langer, S. K. (1957). *Problems of art: Ten philosophical lectures*. Scribner.

Meyer, J. H. F., & Land, R. (2003). Threshold concepts and troublesome knowledge (1): Linkages to ways of thinking and practising within the disciplines. In C. Rust (Ed.), *Improving student learning theory and practice – Ten years on* (pp. 412–424). Oxford Centre for Staff & Learning Development.

Meyer, J. H. F., & Land, R. (2005). Threshold concepts and troublesome knowledge (2): Epistemological considerations and a conceptual framework for teaching and learning. *Higher Education, 49*(3), 373–388. https://doi.org/10.1007/s10734-004-6779-5

Mezirow, J. (1991). *Transformative dimensions of adult learning.* Jossey-Bass.

Mezirow, J. (2000). Learning to think like an adult: Core concepts of transformation theory. In J. Mezirow & Associates (Eds.), *Learning as transformation: Critical perspectives on a theory in progress* (pp. 3–33). Jossey-Bass.

Piaget, J. (1976). Piaget's theory. In B. Inhelder & C. Zwingmann (Eds.), *Piaget and his school: A reader in developmental psychology* (pp. 11–23). Springer.

Pickens, I. B., & Tschopp, N. (2017). *Trauma-informed classrooms.* National Council of Juvenile and Family Court Judges.

Rattray, J. (2016). Affective dimensions of liminality. In R. Land, J. H. F. Meyer, & M. T. Flanagan (Eds.), *Threshold concepts in practice* (pp. 67–76). Sense.

Rogers, C. R. (1983). *Freedom to learn for the 80's.* Merrill.

Ryan, R. M., & Deci, E. L. (2000). Self-determination theory and the facilitation of intrinsic motivation, social development, and well-being. *American Psychologist, 55*(1), 68–78.

SAMHSA. (2016). *Trauma-informed approach and trauma-specific interventions.* Substance Abuse Mental Health Services Administration. http://www.samhsa.gov/nctic/trauma-interventions

Shulman, L. S. (1987). Knowledge and teaching: Foundations of the new reform. *Harvard Educational Review, 57*(1), 1–22.

Smith-Shank, D. L. (1995). Semiotic pedagogy and art education. *Studies in Art Education, 36*(4), 233–241.

Walker, G. (2013). A cognitive approach to threshold concepts. *Higher Education, 65*, 247–263.

Index

accountability movement 3, 17, 18

affective dimension 1, 6, 7, 14, 20, 29, 37, 39–41, 43, 45–50, 54–56, 62, 67, 70, 71, 83, 85, 87, 89, 92, 95, 99, 109–111, 127, 135, 136, 140, 141, 144, 152

arts based research IX, 9–13, 55

a/r/tography IX, X, 53

boundary object 39, 48, 53–55

boundedness 39, 40, 52–54, 142

cognitive dimension 6, 7, 19, 25, 38, 43, 69, 109, 137–140

conceptual portal 1, 37

crisis 117, 118

culturally responsive teaching 6, 28–32, 149

dialogic XVI, 26, 31, 32, 99, 101, 105, 107, 111, 112, 134, 135, 137–140, 148

discursive element 43, 55, 56, 126, 130

emotional safety 30, 39, 48, 92, 145, 146, 150

equity 6, 17, 26, 28–32, 48, 133, 143, 149

gatekeeper 29, 135, 148

identity IX, X, XV, XVI, 3–5, 7, 8, 24, 29, 42, 44, 45, 57, 62–67, 71, 72, 74, 76, 78, 79, 81, 82, 99, 102, 103, 105, 110, 111, 114–119, 121–125, 128, 130, 136, 139, 140, 148

liminal experience 6, 7, 10, 11, 14, 37, 39, 41–45, 50, 54, 57, 91, 105, 115, 126, 127, 130, 135, 136, 141, 143–145, 147, 148, 152

liminal state 2, 6, 11, 13, 37, 41, 43, 45, 48, 50, 51, 53, 56, 70, 71, 83, 84, 89, 91, 97, 103, 107, 109, 110, 118, 125, 133, 134, 136, 137, 140

lived curriculum 148

non-linguistic knowledge 20

ontological shift 4, 7, 9, 42, 43, 49, 50, 51, 62, 82, 89, 91, 96, 97, 109, 114, 119, 123, 128, 133, 134, 136, 139, 147

pedagogy XV–XVII, 2–4, 14, 17, 18, 20, 22, 23, 25–27, 29–31, 41, 42, 46, 48, 57, 133, 135, 137, 140, 143, 144, 147–149, 151, 152

positionality IX, XIII, XVI, XVIII, 28, 30, 144

psychological safety 144, 145, 150

resubjectivity XVI, 122, 147

self IX–XIII, XV, XVI, 1, 2, 4–6, 8, 12, 13, 19, 21, 27, 32, 37–39, 42, 45, 46, 48, 53–57, 62, 63, 65–67, 69, 71, 77–79, 81–83, 85–90, 95, 96, 99–101, 103, 105, 107–112, 114–128, 130, 131, 134–143, 145, 148, 151

self dialogue 55, 56, 95, 110

semiotics 22, 25, 27, 62, 141, 144, 146

semiotic pedagogy 27, 29, 41, 46, 48, 57, 135, 137, 143, 144, 148, 152

stuck place 37, 41, 50, 110, 117, 126, 136, 137

student centered 17, 30, 31, 145

tacit 40, 49–51, 53, 54, 56, 71, 107, 111, 134, 135, 137, 138, 140, 141, 146, 148, 150, 152

threshold concepts IX, X, XIII, 1, 2, 4, 5, 7, 11–14, 17, 18, 30–33, 37–41, 43, 45, 46, 50, 51, 53, 55, 57, 89, 103, 115, 117, 133–136, 141, 142, 144, 146, 148, 151, 152

threshold crossing XVIII, 1, 2, 5, 37–43, 46, 55, 56, 89, 91, 96, 107, 109, 111, 114, 119, 126, 129, 130, 138, 141, 142

transformative IX, XVI, 1, 7, 12, 20, 22, 25, 27, 31, 37–39, 41, 42, 48, 49, 54, 103, 107, 114, 130, 134, 140, 152

trauma informed classrooms 6, 145

troublesome knowledge IX, XVIII, 1, 9, 11, 22, 26, 37, 40, 46, 48, 50, 51, 56, 57, 63, 89, 99, 117, 121, 133–136, 140, 143, 145, 147, 152

troublesomeness XV, 4, 26, 40, 41, 44, 45, 50, 53, 64, 69, 81, 89, 97, 110, 112, 134, 139

visual culture X, 22–24, 31

visual language XVI, 20–22, 27, 32, 33, 42, 56, 115, 127, 130, 136–138, 140, 142, 146, 147

visual literacy 17, 22–25, 27, 31

voice X, 12, 51, 57, 81–83, 86, 88–91, 95, 96, 110–112, 114, 119, 122, 123, 128, 129, 134–136, 139, 140, 148

Printed in the United States
by Baker & Taylor Publisher Services